the RADICAL Self-Expert

The Fastest Simplest 7 Step Method to Discover How to Be Your True Self, Change Your Life NOW & Be Happy TODAY!~ The Easy Way!

Tiphanie Jamison VanDerLugt, Esq.

The Yay Me University ISBN: 13: 978-0615742663
ISBN: 10: 0615742661
For print or media interviews with Tiphanie please contact: ***Press@TheYayMeUniversity.com***

Tiphanie Jamison VanDerLugt
Telephone: 1 (760) 565-3106
Email: ***Tiphanie@TheYayMeUniversity.com***

Limits of Liability and Disclaimer of Warranty:
The author and publisher shall not be liable for your misuse of this material. This book is strictly for informational and educational purposes only. It is not intended to replace or substitute any advice from your medical practitioner, a qualified doctor, attorney, therapist or any other professional and advisor. You should consult a qualified health practitioner before implementing any of the suggestions found in this book and should not give up any medical treatment you are using without the express consent of a medical professional. For diagnosis or treatment of a medical condition contact your own physician.

The author and/or publisher do not guarantee that anyone following these techniques, suggestions, tips, ideas, or strategies will become successful. The author and/or publisher shall have neither liability nor responsibility to anyone with respect to any loss or damage caused, or alleged to be caused, directly or indirectly by the information contained in this book. References are provided for informational purposes only and do not constitute endorsement of any website or sources. This book is sold with the express understanding that the author and publisher are not rendering medical, health, or personal services. The author and publisher disclaim all liability associated with the recommendations and guidelines set forth in this book.

DEDICATION

"Here's to the crazy ones, the misfits, the rebels, the troublemakers, the round pegs in the square holes... the ones who see things differently -- they're not fond of rules... You can quote them, disagree with them, glorify or vilify them, but the only thing you can't do is ignore them because they change things... they push the human race forward, and while some may see them as the crazy ones, we see genius, because the ones who are crazy enough to think that they can change the world, are the ones who do." Steve Jobs

Table of Contents

PREFACE

Haven't you always known that there is something more than what you are experiencing right now?

How long will you wait and watch others feast off the joys of life, while you sit there with the indigestion?

"You never change things by fighting the existing reality. To change something, build a new model that makes the existing model obsolete."
Richard Buckminster Fuller

YAY! I am so honored that you have taken the time to get my book. I love the Richard Buckminster Fuller quote because it speaks to the aim of this book. **This book is NOT another positive thinking, motivational, "feel good" book that** will elevate you like a sugar high, and in a few hours/days/weeks (when the sugar high wears off), send you crashing back to earth.

In fact, I would even be so audacious to say, that this book is not for you and you should stop reading if any of the following apply to you:

a) You are invested and committed to feeling and being permanently and irreparably "broken"...
b) Don't want your days full of YAYYYY!!!!
c) Don't desire to easily and instantly experience and KNOW YOUR OWN TRUTH...
d) Aren't interested in a life of freedom, space, joy, and ease...
e) Persist in setting "SMART" goals, even though you are not getting results...
f) Want to dredge up, relive and feel, everything in your past in order to "change" it...
g) Don't want to challenge your current assumptions...
h) Don't want to take control of your life...
i) Want to continue to struggle to find, happiness, fulfillment, purpose and money as a way to prove you deserve and are worthy of it...
j) Looking for more and exciting ways to create a vision board and write new affirmations as the means to "manifest" the life of your dreams.
k) Believe that there is a "right" way to be spiritual and that

any other way is "wrong"...

l) Are addicted to positive thinking, yet are still not getting the results in your life you want…
m) Believe that where you are, is ALL there is or ever will be…
n) Committed and advocate conventional wisdom.
o) Don't want to grow, have or be everything you were designed to be….
p) Looking for more tools and tactics to "fix" the old model of you…
q) Want to keep life as hard as possible to show your strength…
r) Only purpose in life is to sacrifice your happiness, mind, body, soul and potential, to show you are a "good" person…
s) Want to be told what to think, do and be.
t) Want to be told what is "right" for you to do, think and be…
u) Don't want to be powerful…
v) Don't want to find comfort in and love all of you…
w) Want to stay in judgment of you and everything around you…

Can you imagine how you will feel knowing, how to trust yourself, experience improved health, wealth and freedom with ease? Wouldn't it just be wonderful, to love all of you, and not see yourself through the eyes of others; to not judge yourself, as wrong, bad, incapable or "got issues". Aren't you just over living someone else's life and calling it yours?

What I am inviting you to do through this book, is to make that whole just "feel good, positive thinking, "woo-woo with the same go do" model of changing things in your life obsolete; The time for you to design the new model of you just for you, is NOW!

As you read this book, you will begin to have space in your mind, heart, and body, that you never dreamed possible. It will be as if you are seeing everything for the first time. Just be open, allow the peace and possibilities that are open for you to wash over you like an awesome warm mist of energy. Allow it to fill every part of you, from the top of your head to the soles of your feet. See that energy stretch out in every direction, around the world and back again. You can do it! I am proof of what's possible and I have helped countless others do the same.

What is a Radical Self-Expert? RADICAL, is an easy, powerful, practical step by step method to dynamically and dramatically change every area of your life, that isn't working for you, instantly. Each letter represents a step in that Method. As for being a Self-Expert, I define that below.

Self \\` self\\ n. the essential person distinct from all other persons in identity

+

Expert \\ `ek- spərt\\ adj. showing special skill or knowledge

Put it all together- RADICAL is the tool, to enable you to honor your unique truth, distinct from all other persons in identity to facilitate and access specialized knowledge in YOU. YAY! How RAD is that?

I am so excited to share this with you!

In order to get the most out of this book, my recommendation is that you keep a journal and fully participate in the action steps. Reading is an awesome place to begin your transformation, but change can only come through new action. Information only becomes knowledge when it is applied. This book is yours and I want you to receive incredible life transforming value. You are the answer to unlocking every block, barrier, doubt, fear and/or obstacle in your life.

Becoming a Radical Self-Expert is the bridge, between what you witness is possible with others and what you actually experience is possible for you. I am sure that at some time in your life, you have been to a workshop, taken a course, or even had someone report back his/her quantum success and thought to yourself…"I went to that workshop… I used those tools, why didn't it work for me?"

Being a Radical Self-Expert means that you not only know what you know, but you know THAT you know the answers to your life's questions in any given situation or circumstance. My intention is to share with you, how to be an Expert in YOU…

This is not to suggest that you won't acquire information from other sources, you absolutely will. We should all have a "council of learned advisors". The thing is, when you are more dialed into your unique truth, the things outside of you, (i.e. opinions, diagnosis, suggestions, beliefs) are JUST data, no more, no less.

Your Self-Expertise, will guide you to use the data as part of your decision making or not, take action or not. You will have fail-safe tools, to know what is true for you and either use or throw it away with confidence and ease.

By the end of this book, you will be a RADICAL Self- Expert, which is the most important tool to having the life you were always destined for; A life full of love, personal power, wealth, happiness and beyond. It is possible I am proof of what is possible. Are you ready?

As Mr. Fuller so eloquently points out, that the only way to truly change something, is by making the “old something” (model) obsolete.

The New Model of You won’t involve more sameness of typical self-help, personal growth, and motivational books. I will not tell you what to think or how to be, or about healing your shadows from the past. You will not use the typical tools, such as affirmations, vision boards, Tibetan meditations, reliving the past or intense quasi-therapeutic sessions to create a new version of you. Heck, I did all of those things and then some, with very few results (if I may be so transparent).

While I think each of those tools may be helpful to some, they have their place and use, but not necessarily in the way that we have been trained to use them; more on that later in the book.

Introduction

That moment in time, when the "fog" lifts, and things become clear, is always oddly magical. The fog cleared for me after the loss of 5 babies, (I call them my Lost Angels) in a row from early 2007 to summer of 2008. Prior to the losses of those babies, I was consuming every self-help book and personal growth approach I could find, but nothing seemed to "stick". Oh sure, I would get a motivation boost here, and little inspiration there, but nothing permanent and lasting. It was almost as if, there was a quasi-addiction to the "figuring it out and fixing me."

Professionally, I was "'successful" by everyone else's standards. I had my own law practice, a house, a few bucks in the bank and could (basically) come and go as I pleased. Despite all of those things, I was still "lonely" and wanted desperately to find love. I wanted that feeling of "this isn't working" to go away. So what does one do when they are emotionally messed up?? Yep, they go looking for love. Not always the most optimum time, right? Live and learn.

In search of the that "something" to fill that gapping whole in my heart, I did what most busy professional lonely people do, I joined an internet dating site.

At that time, leaving my law practice was deemed unthinkable, so dating anyone other than a man around the corner, was not in my plan. Much to my surprise, and lack of local prospects, I went trolling the sites for some international flavors. Well, there he was- tall, blonde hair and blue eyed.

I was so not interested, but thought, he had great eyes. Perhaps, he could be a pen pal, or I could have a place to stay if/when I could get away from my practice and visit Europe.

Well, suffice it to say, that this man, now known as Frederik (I named him "Dutch") sent me a message, saying, "finally my dream woman". I thought, "well, isn't that cute". He requested my personal email, which I hesitated to give, and we began chatting.

Being the Taurus that he is, he PUSHED full steam ahead and after a couple of days of chatting, he professed his undying love for me, and announced his was coming for a visit. I was like, HUH? I must admit that I did not take him seriously, and quickly dismissed the notion of a foreign stranger coming to California for me.

Well, after a few more weeks of chatting, he had booked a flight and enrolled my then assistant and (one of my favorite people on the planet) in a plan to propose on my birthday. On March 1, 2007, he flew into LAX, March 2, 2007, he proposed and by March 6, 2007, I was Mrs. VanDerLugt; only I had no idea how to pronounce my new name.

Notwithstanding the fact, that I was clearly not in my right mind, one thing we were both certain of (or so I thought and was led to believe) , was the desire for more children. Perhaps on some level, the drive for children kept us together through some very trying times that were ahead for us.

From the honeymoon, baby making was on the brain. What am I saying? It was on it, in it, around it, it was ALL there was. If it was only that easy, right?

As I discuss throughout this book, success in my fertility demanded that I not only be a quasi-fertility expert, but more importantly, be an expert in me. I had to get clear, on what is or is not true for me.

During my "fertility journey" aka, *"the baby quest",* I was living someone else's truth instead of my own. All of the fears, thoughts, and beliefs that were guiding my choices and creating so much inner contempt and hatred, were not mine, but rather the programming and conditioning of my environment, family, "friends" and the like.

While the first 3 losses were beyond painful, it was the loss of my Twin Angels that sent me reeling. The Twin Angels were post-the movie the Secret. I had my vision board, affirmations, and was "feeling good" and still lost those babies in traumatic and dramatic fashion. What the hell, right? This law of attraction stuff was on Oprah, who was like the Patron Saint of Personal Growth-meaning, the stuff should "work", right?

Thomas Jefferson, a Self-Help Guru?

Then it happened. I love history, and I happened to be watching a television series chronicling the American Revolution. There was a quote by Thomas Jefferson. He stated, "Our properties within our own territories [should not] be taxed or regulated by any power on earth but our own."

You are probably thinking, "How in the heck does that relate to changing your life Tiph?" In that moment, I reflected over ALL of the decisions I made regarding my life, my lost Angels, my toxic family, the doctors, teachers, the ex, past relationships, self-help gurus, everything.

Thomas Jefferson may have been referring to freeing America from British Rule, but I wanted to free myself of other people's "rule". Certainly, I was free (not a slave), however, I was relying on other people's promises, and opinions of how great my life would be, if I did what they did, said, told me; I was governed by things outside of myself but calling it my life.

My "TERRITORY" i.e. ME, was being regulated by other powers. I was in bondage! Keep reading because there is much more to come regarding declaring your own revolution.

Bondage is – subjection to external influences and internal negative thoughts and attitudes. W. Clement Stone

For Jefferson, it was land, and tangible goods, that he felt should be governed only by Americans. In my case, the property, the territory was my life- my happiness, babies, peace of mind, freedom, and love.

Now I Ask YOU...

Who or What Is Governing YOUR Territory?

Each of the lost angels was painful, yet it was after the loss of my Twin Angels, despite doing tons of affirmations, vision boards, meditations, visualizations, and "being positive", I declared my own personal revolution. I felt there was some "truth" and efficacy to those things, but I was still not experiencing the "Genie in the Bottle" results as promised by the Secret and I knew it was my time to lovingly revolt.

"All the higher, more penetrating ideals are revolutionary."
William James

I declared a Revolution, which led to my Reality Nouveau.

Reality *\rē al i tē-\ n. The State or Quality of Being Real*
Nouveau *\nū'vō, nū-vō'\, adj. Newly or recently created, or come into prominence*

As I learned more about how the "I" fit into my life, I realized, I was the only person strong enough to stop me from the life I desired; AND I was the only one powerful enough to set me free.

And so… the Fastest Simplest 7 Step Method to Discover How to Be Your True Self, Change Your Life Now and Be Happy Today-The Easy Way! Was born….

So it began, my quest to make the old model of transformation, creation, and having the things that I desired, obsolete; replacing it with something that would work for my fertility and later anything else I desired to have, be or experience. Rather than elevating someone else to the status of "expert" in my life, I decided to BE MY OWN SELF-EXPERT, a RADICAL SELF-EXPERT that is!

We were born into this world a UNIQUE MODEL of individuality, knowing everything there is or ever will be to know, about ourselves. Who on earth, could possibly know more about you, than you? Yet, for reasons discussed in this book, we neither celebrate nor embrace our greatest power which is our uniqueness. Instead, we subvert, suppress and deny it to our spiritual detriment, self-fulfillment, true desires and happiness.

You deserve, or rather were DESTINED to live your unique truth. In the words of Johann Wolfgang von Goethe, ***"If God had wanted me otherwise, He would have created me otherwise."*** Call it God, Source, the Universe, Mother Earth, Shaman, Your Higher Self, Shinto, whatever resonates with you. Your power lies in you knowing, experiencing and acting on what you know, AND to KNOW that YOU KNOW what is true for you.

You will find that I often refer to my fertility journey [Baby Quest] and/or pregnancies, because it was my turning point. For you, it may the loss of a loved one or relationship. Perhaps, it is an illness or divorce, substitute whatever the "thing" is in your life right now that you are facing or have faced. The magic of being a RADICAL

Self-Expert, is that the Method can be applied in any situation, to accomplish what is seemingly impossible. I used it to overcome the pain of infertility, childhood abuse and neglect, failed relationships, "bad" decisions, judgments, self-hatred, and loss to finally creating the peace of mind that eluded me for 30+ years.

What I know, and want you to know, is there is NOTHING wrong with you.

You are NOT broken.

You aren't doing the "self-help, positive thinking thing" wrong. It isn't the vision board (or lack of one) or not meditating for 2 hours a day like a Tibetan Monk, that keeps you stuck, feeling hopeless and wrong. You don't have to be more forgiving, beg God for mercy, make sacrifices or become "good" to have everything you desire. YOU are enough, just as you are; unfortunately, you have just been using tools, that aren't tailored for all of your "uniqueness".

If you have made it this far, I know that YOU and I were meant to be here together. Are you ready to live, love, rock the world as only you can??? YAY!!!!

STEP 1. R= REALITY NOUVEAU

Reality \rē al i tē-\ n. The State or Quality of Being Real

Nouveau \nū'vō, nū-vō'\, adj. Newly or recently created, developed or come into prominence

"Let us live for the beauty of our own reality." Charles Lamb
"I reject your reality and substitute it for my own." Adam Savage

The Self-Help Trifecta...Working Harder but Getting Nowhere?

Are you currently using what I call the *"Self-Help Trifecta"* as the means by which to create and/or achieve greater health, wealth, happiness, and success in some or all areas of your life? What in the heck, is the *Self-Help Trifecta,* you say? Awesome question! The *"Self-Help Trifecta"*, are the traditional or conventional self-help/ personal development tools, that are promoted and taught by the self-help industry consisting of- (1) the Positives- affirmations positive self-talk and positive thinking; (2) knowing your "big why"; and (3) the "success" mindset.

According to the proponents of the "Self-Help Trifecta", positive thinking and affirmations are the most effective means by which to change your life.

How many times have you read about "limiting beliefs" and removing negative blocks? I submit that the Self-Help Trifecta is a form of limitation as well.

Sort of a trip, right? The thing that is supposed to liberate us, is actually keeping us stuck...More on that proposition later.

The effectiveness of the Self-Help Trifecta greatly depends on some unreasonable assumptions and/or does not take into account a variety of things, specifically:

1. It assumes- at some point in your life, you had at least some minimally functional role models. (Teachers, grandparents, caregivers, principal, guidance counselor).
2. Your past is not replete with abuse, neglect, and trauma of varying degrees.
3. You are not deeply religious as well as taking into account, how your religious beliefs factor in to the personal growth or lack thereof. (Note: There is a distinction between being religious and being spiritual. By religious, I am referring to the traditional organized religion(s).
4. That if you did have a history of neglect and abuse- somehow you come to the *Self-Help Trifecta,* "pre-helped" via therapy, counseling, or some other healing work.
5. That you know, use, and actively follow your intuition.
6. You are in tune with yourself and what your feelings mean; you have a clear sense of who you are.

7. That you have at least normal self-esteem.
8. Thatyourenvironment,Ireferto thisastheANGLESof Influence (AOI) is either supportive or (minimally) is not a hindrance to yourgrowth.
9. That you have a lot of friends and/or family members that are not threatened by your growth, or are not invested in the status quo, i.e. things staying the same.
10. Your mind is a clean unencumbered place, with space to pour in positive stuff.

These are but some of the assumptions that are never fully addressed by the *Self-Help Trifecta*. The irony is that, the people who use the *Self-Help Trifecta*, are those most in need. Yet their needs are mostly being addressed by assumptions. Crazy, right? I am sure you've read a book, heard a guru speak about choice pushing yourself harder, or being more motivated, etc. If just doing more was the problem, then the whole industry would cease to exist.

How many books, DVDs, products, seminars, workshops, and episodes of Dr. Phil and Oprah have you watched? I know I have watched more than my share and implemented all of it on some level- excluding those things that were simply not applicable.

Let's Take a Closer Look at the Self-Help Trifecta Positive Thinking & Affirmations

Positive Thinking

An interesting study conducted by the University of Waterloo and University of New Brunswick concluded that positive self-statements are ineffective.[1] What was particularly interesting was the fact that positive statements, were not only ineffective for the people who "needed" them (people with lower self-esteem) positive self-statements were actually harmful. YIKES! Here is an excerpt from the study:

> *"Injunctions to "think positively" are pervasive in North America. Self-help books, television shows, and loved ones advise thinking positively when one faces a challenge or is unhappy. Yet the present results suggest that for certain people, positive self-statements may be not only ineffective, but actually detrimental. When people with low self-esteem repeated the statement, "I'm a lovable person" (Study 2), or focused on ways in which this statement was true of them (Study 3), neither their feelings about themselves nor their moods improved—they got worse. Positive self-statements seemed to provide a boost only to people with high self- esteem—those who ordinarily feel good about themselves already—and that boost was small.*[2]

Joanne V. Wood, one of the psychologists conducting the study, determined that by asking people with low self- esteem to focus exclusively on positive thoughts, those same people not only found it difficult to block negative ones, but ultimately felt their negative self-opinions became more deeply engrained. Further, they felt because they were "unsuccessful" at blocking negative thoughts, they were "less than" and didn't measure up to others.

Naturally, this runs counter to everything we are taught about how to change our lives, right? We are told, especially after the phenomenon that was the Secret, to think positive, expect good things, and magic will happen.

What I now understand, by examining my own circumstances, and the people that I have helped- positive thinking alone, has little to anything to do with creating, experiencing, and being the life that you desire. It sort of makes sense right? How many people do you know, that are negative thinkers with less than sunny dispositions who have been extremely successful in various areas of their lives? Heck, I can think of a few right now. Can you think of anyone that has less than a positive attitude and seems to have the Midas touch?

I am by no means suggesting that positive thinking and affirmations aren't helpful. What I invite you to consider is that positive thinking and affirmations are not the panacea of changing your life. I want to offer you a more effective, efficient way to easily and instantly change your life.

Affirmations

I was once a huge fan of affirmations. Even when I would achieve inconsistent results, I would try again, to get them "just right", so that I could be the thing I was affirming. Affirmations in and of themselves create an inner struggle that may further lock in place the limiting beliefs you are trying to clear. I am sure you know what I am talking about.

While affirmations have the best of intentions, they sort of run counter to how the minds of those who need them work. Affirmations create an internal conflict that at times creates more of the things you don't want. During my fertility struggle, I was told by a guru, to affirm that I was "fertile". When I would look in the mirror and say that to myself, a (large) part of my mind, said, "Bullsh#t!...if I was fertile, I wouldn't have lost all of those babies".

When you do affirmations, it's like, if someone walks up to you, and tells you are wearing jeans when you are wearing a dress; your mind, immediately says, "I'm not wearing jeans, I'm wearing a dress, you idiot.'

I will share much more constructive efficient ways to use affirmations that create less internal resistance in the "C" of RADICAL. For now, ask yourself honestly, have affirmations been ***consistently*** effective in creating the life that you desire.

Now, my aim is not to offend those of you that swear by affirmations, positive thinking, and the like. Heck, if that's how you roll, I will only say YAY!

However, for those of us, who have spent and/or are spending thousands of dollars and hundreds of hours on going to every personal development workshop, doing, and redoing the perfect vision board so we can finally get results, we need to start a REVOLUTION and create a Reality Nouveau. If we are doing everything that, the "gurus" say we should, and we are not experiencing the results, then IT IS TIME FOR A NEW MODEL.

Let's Take a Look at the "Big Why"

You are told, that when you know your "big why", you will then move forward- your big why is sort of the catalyst for your life change and success, right? There are many people, who can articulate why they would want what they want.

Think about it...

How many people can you think of, say they want to release excess weight, because they want to be healthier, happier, live longer, have children, be with their families, etc. ? Yet, they are not able to release the excess weight permanently, if at all? They yo-yo diet, or use extreme measures to release weight, only to find themselves back where they started… but at least they knew their "big why", right? Worse still, because they knew their "big why" and weren't successful, their "big why" becomes this "big shiny symbol and reminder" of their failures. The "big why", ends up further sinking their spirit and self-esteem. Instead of their "big why" propelling them forward as promised, it has them falling deeper into an emotional, and spiritual quicksand.

The assumption with the "big why" is that it is YOUR why. Here is the problem. Much if not all of your judgments, conclusions opinions and beliefs are not even yours. Perhaps your "big why" is based on things you have been told, or conditioned to believe you "should" be doing, or have judged to be acceptable. Your so-called "big why", may be the why of *someone else.*

No, I am not talking about the old cliché, "define success for yourself." It is so much deeper than merely defining success. In the second step of RADICAL we will take a deep dive into how 97% of what we think and feel are not truly our own feelings; for now, it is only important that your why, actually be truly **your why.**

A "why" that is uniquely yours, rather than something you have heard, handed down, trained in, or been lead to believe and have been operating from. The "why" that is not based upon a conclusion or judgment of what is right or wrong. A why, not from the limitations of your current circumstances, but the why you were born with... overflowing with joy, possibility and excited expectancy.

Again, as with positive thinking and affirmations, the "big why" has its place in the ever evolving you. However, it is important to be an expert on you, so that your why is actually "YOUR WHY", and not the why of your those that are having the greatest influence on your life- i.e. the thoughts, feelings, judgments, beliefs, and the like, of others... aka the ANGLES of Influence (AOI). Again, we will get into ANGLES in the A of RADICAL.

And Finally- The Success Mindset

So to be successful we are told to develop and/or have a success mindset like "successful people". Among others, there are a number of challenges with this proposition but I will be discussing four (4).

(1) The idea that thinking like someone else, will make you successful does not recognize that the key gift to your life, is YOUR uniqueness. Further, it connotes that your ability to think for yourself and from yourself, is somehow wrong thereby making the other person "right". Ultimately, this creates a greater feeling of inferiority and a profound feeling of "wrongness". It starts to become a never ending cycle of "trying to be like". You start to believe that in order to have, be or do something, you have to

do it the way "they" did it; You have to meditate the way, "they" meditate, you have to visualize the way "they visualize", your vision board, has to look a certain way, you have to have a certain mentor. Notice how all of those things are OUTWARD looking? Where is there room for your uniqueness to be expressed? You will always be looking to "be like" someone else and never step into the power of you. Sadly when "being like" invariably breaks down, you feel worse than when you started, because you couldn't "keep it up". It is maddening.

(2) If you are not an expert in you, you may become outwardly successful, but inwardly a "failure", which will lead to sadness, depression and loneliness.

(3) If you have never had success, how in the world would you even know what a success mindset is...? And

(4) You will NEVER have the mindset of a particular person, because we are ALL unique. Albert Einstein's mindset was not like Nikola Tesla or Thomas Edison- All geniuses, all inventors, but VERY different mindsets. There were some similarities, in their use of the other keys; I speak of later in this book. However, none of them had the same mindset- and that is why they were successful. Not because they copied others, but because they honored themselves.

Thomas Edison would easily be characterized as the "hard working" inventor; Whereas, Tesla, was more of a visualizing strategist. Albert Einstein, was big on imagination and curiosity... Each inventor possessing amazing mindsets- each with a different approach to everything; each of them using their unique innate gifts and greatness.

Now, no one would dare go to Tesla and say, "...although you are this wonderful inventor, you need to be more like Edison, he is a hard worker." Why would they? For Tesla to work harder, would mean that his truth and gifts would not be expressed. How could he then bring forth something great? He would always be lacking, trying to be like someone else. Get it? Of course you do. My suspicion is that you have known this all the time.

Based on many traditional self-help books, a success mindset encompasses seven (7) elements give or take:

1. desire;
2. commitment;
3. responsibility;
4. hard work;
5. positive belief;
6. self-belief &
7. persistence

As noted in the prior discussion of the “Old Model”, positive thinking and self-talk, are not necessarily as effective in changing people’s lives as some believe. I unfortunately, know of too many people who (for lack of knowing any other way to be) persist and are committed to being unhappy. They also desire something more and work hard, but cannot seem to make any headway in life.

I submit that rather than attempting to unsuccessfully develop a “success mindset”, what would be more effective would be to develop your Self-Expertise. If we are born perfect with our unique gifts completely intact, then going back to that uniqueness and amplifying it, just makes sense, right? What is true for one mindset is NOT true for another. Saying otherwise, is well, simply a lie. Bill Gates, did not think like the late Steve Jobs. Michael Jordon doesn’t think like Magic Johnson or Larry Bird. They all celebrated and created an environment to expand their uniqueness and were consequently successful.

Trying to be positive, persistent, committed, have desire, and work hard all at the same time, will invariably keep you running but going nowhere. How do any of those things lead DIRECTLY to what is your unique truth? What they do, is mask your truth, by keeping you busy with the external things of persistence, positive thoughts, affirmations and the like.

The funny thing is, the touted tools to develop the "success mindset" involve the very things that have been scientifically proven to be marginally successful at best and detrimental at worst. In other words, the foundational principles are flawed. We know that a flawed foundation can only lead to a flawed structure, right?

Think about it this way- Would you buy a house from someone when you KNOW the foundation is cracked? HECK NO!

As you spin on this wheel of trying to develop a "success mindset", you buy another book or attend another workshop, that will help you get "the missing piece", right? If you could just be more positive, use better affirmations, work harder, you will have the necessary "success mindset", that will open the treasure trove of life and be happy. You see that author, guru, TV host as "right" and yourself as "wrong" and further devalue (the most important thing in your life), YOU. What I want you to know is that your mindset is already successful. You just have to access what you know and that you know.

While gathering information and observing successful people can be helpful lasting financial, spiritual, emotional, physical and psychological abundance can flow only from who YOU are truly. Certainly, you gather data from external sources. For example, Magic Johnson had a coach that helped him become "Magic", but that coach didn't say, dribble like me, think like me. He looked at Magic's unique gifts and enhanced what was already there.

The "Success Mindset" is this incessant cycle of outward data gathering, failed application and renewed quest for more outward data gathering. You learn a particular modality, thinking it will "work" for you as it has for others, apply it, fail (not because of lack of effort, but it just being a modality that was not "true" for you), then you start looking again for another modality that will work.

In fact, I know that I would go from guru to guru, looking for "the answer" to "fix" my mindset to be successful. What I ultimately figured out, was the guru was me- just as your guru is you. With the Radical Self-Expert Method, you have easy tools to assess what is true for you, and then take action that is in support of your truth. There is no one size fit all. Your personal development and growth is Haute Couture (/ˌoʊt kuːˈtʊər/), tailored made, just for you.

Your mindset is the success mindset, once you free it from conventional wisdom, Angles and AOI. How much more time are you going to give to the old model (of you) ...weeks, months, years? Relating to my own circumstance, I wanted a baby, and I wanted one yesterday; so time was of the essence. I refused to give what wasn't working another Nano-second. As far as I was concerned, I would not spend another nickel on more of the same information on how to be happy by thinking positive, saying affirmations, and creating a "better" vision board.

Why would I? How many more affirmations and vision boards was it going to take before I got my babies? More poignantly, how many more babies would I have to lose before I was willing to say, "F- this", this is not working for me. I wasn't willing to lose one more baby in the name of conventional wisdom, vision boards or positive thinking. Just to be clear, all of those tools have a place in getting desired results for your life; just not in the conventional way we have been taught to use them.

Aren't you ready to start reaping the harvest of all of your personal development work?

Again, each modality in the Self-Help Trifecta, has its place in personal development. In fact, the Self-Help Trifecta will be used to help facilitate your Self-Expertise, which you will experience later in the book.

"Revolution is not the uprising against preexisting order, but the setting up of a new order contradictory to the traditional one." Jose Ortega y Gasset

YOUR PERSONAL REVOLUTION AND REALITY NOUVEAU

Part of being a Radical, is starting your own Revolution. That means, to change, everything you have made "right", "wrong", "good" or "bad", all of your judgments, conclusions, assumptions, everything that you have aligned and agreed with and/or resisted and reacted to... those things that you have been taught, programmed and conditioned to be, the conventional self-help tools, surface level positive thinking, everything! Why not change, right? It isn't like you are getting the consistently wonderful results.

Your revolution is essential to you creating your Reality Nouveau. What is true for you, is ONLY true for you, no matter how much you seek to identify with and connect to the truths of others.

Perhaps you are not looking for babies, perhaps you have a business, are an entrepreneur, or looking for love. Start your REVOLUTION to create your *Reality Nouveau.*

Promise yourself to live your life as a revolution and not just a process of evolution. ~Anthony J. D'Angelo

In order to be a RADICAL Self-Expert, you must break away from the crowd, peers, and conventional wisdom. You can only begin to see what is possible, when you free yourself from the perspective of others. The choice for each and every one of us, is whether we allow societal norms, beliefs, conclusions, judgments, thoughts and feelings, handed down from our families and other AOI to dictate our grandest visions of the extraordinary life we desire.

We only become what we are by the radical and deep-seated refusal of that which others have made of us.
Jean-Paul Sartre

Declare your independence. You have but one life, so in the mold of the great Thomas Jefferson, declare YOUR truths to be self-evident, and while all women are created equal, that you are endowed by YOUR Creator, with your own innate awareness, uniqueness and TRUTH from which you are Free to BE!

"Revolutions never go backwards" Proverb

If you are using the Self-Help Trifecta and your days are overflowing with YAY, then wonderful and YAY for you.
My suspicion, is that if you are reading this book, you are looking for something more than what you have been doing; You see and feel that there is more for you to be, do or have- be it more money, happiness, relationships, love, a successful business, or peace of mind.

If you are so "over" more vision boarding, positive thinking, affirmations, meditations and the like, and are not achieving the massive quantum leaps as promised, then start your revolution that will create your Reality Nouveau. A Reality Nouveau that was made for you, by you and ONLY for you. From this place, you can give so much more to the world.

What is the cost to you, continuing in your old reality-the old model of you? Where will you be 6 months from now, doing exactly what you are doing? You have waited long enough. Your time is NOW!

You are intelligent enough to know, that if you keep doing what you are doing, you will keep getting what you are getting. As Einstein pointed out, doing the same things and expecting different results is the very definition of insanity. The law of polarity says, for everything on the planet, there is an opposite; meaning for every cold there is a hot, for every up there is a down.

In this case, for every hard way, there has to be an **easier way**. I know you are ready to experience an easier way. You deserve it. Let go of the past, I am offering you the greatest gift on earth, your freedom to be you. Declare your personal revolution of thought. You ARE NOT broken, and don't need to be fixed

ACTION STEP:

Ask yourself who and what is governing your territory.

Based upon your unique personal growth and development experiences, what modalities, tips, tricks, techniques and tools have you used to achieve the results you desire in your life? What has been most effective? What have been the challenges with each of those tools?

Are you ready, willing and excited to create your Reality Nouveau?

Will you declare your Revolution?

Step 2. A= ANGLES…

ANGLES of Influence, Creation, Energy and Resonance

Our ideas, like orange-plants, spread out in proportion to the size of the box which imprisons the roots. Edward Bulwer Lytton

A. ANGLES –*Defined….*

"Everyone is born a genius, but the process of living de-geniuses them." R. Buckminster Fuller

Remember how in the cartoons, when Bugs Bunny would get an idea, a light bulb would appear over his head and the sound of a bell would go off? That's exactly what happened to me, after my personal revolution. I was in the shower, when I heard "the ding". In a flash, the answer was so clear. For those people with "less baggage", putting up a vision board, and some positive self-talk, may prove quite effective. For those of us, with emotional baggage that is so heavy that a 747 jet couldn't carry it, something a little more ninja style would be in order to create the massive change I wanted.

After my revolution, I kept asking, "if not that, then what? What is it going to take to get the sh*# I want?"

I was standing in the shower and a flood of questions starting pouring into my mind. It was like the matrix or something. One question that kept coming up was, "what's different?" How is it, or what is it that makes some people make the shift while the rest of us, despite our best efforts, books, workshops, seminars, and episodes of Oprah don't? Or at our best are, "less negative" and at our worst, broke, unhappy and bordering on hopeless.

I applied this "mindset stuff" to every situation I could think of. Of course, my baby quest was top of mind. I examined the different mindsets of women with infertility challenges versus women who ultimately overcame infertility issues.

To get better clarity and distance from such a "hot" issue, I applied it to money, passing the California bar exam (finally) and relationships. Applying my key question to other less emotionally charged topics for me, crystallized the key distinction, between those who "make the shift" and those who are diligently languishing in neutral.

I now know, what sets apart a self-made millionaire from a lottery millionaire, or an athlete that makes millions with his athletic prowess. Make no mistake; there is a clear and identifiable distinction between someone who attends (a personal or business development) workshop and gets results versus someone who doesn't get results. There is a difference between those who are the "testimonials" after using the latest information product and the "regulars" on the get rich quick, "frequent attender" workshop circuit.

I ask you, do you think there is a difference between the person that makes 10,000 dollars per week and the person who is in 10,000 dollars in debt (other than the money itself)?

ANGLES...

ANGLES distinguish the mother of 5 healthy children from the (desperately wanting) mother of none. They distinguish Warren Buffett from the lucky lottery winner or millionaire athlete- More on this later.

When I refer to ANGLES, I am referring to those points of view(s) that each of us are programmed, conditioned, or taught and later buy as our own. Those unexamined behaviors that we visually refer to as "habits" or "family traditions- Including, but not limited to, the secret, invisible, covert, unseen, hidden, unheard, unacknowledged thoughts, behaviors, beliefs and decisions that are made each and every moment.

Generally, we are not even aware of how ANGLES are creating our reality. We have concluded erroneously, that "that is just the way things are", or "some people are just born lucky", or "all men cheat", "or only if ...then..."

Now, I ask you, do you go around each day, consciously (on the surface saying to yourself) that "all men are abusers" or "I love being broke". Of course not, you say things like, "I want a man that is nice to me... or I wished I had more money". You put it up on your vision board and everything, right? So, if your ANGLE, is that you want a man that is nice to you, or you want more money and you don't have that, there is a glaring disconnect between what you say, and your reality, right? More on this to follow shortly.

You may have heard the word ANGLE used in journalism to refer to a journalist's point of view; his/her slant or take on the story. ANGLE(S) is the word I use to refer to our points of view from which our reality is created. While in many ways I use points of view and ANGLES interchangeably, I think ANGLES are much more limiting than points of view. ANGLES are very defined, in scope, direction, perception, and can always be measured. By definition, an ANGLE is finite. This is precisely, the effect ANGLES have on the possibilities to live, have and be everything we deserve and desire. They can be measured with precision. So as our ANGLES go, so does the life we currently live.

We "buy" other people's ANGLES by aligning, agreeing, resisting, or reacting to them, in any way. It could be conscious, by judging something as either "right" or "wrong", "good or bad", or accidentally, as the case with aligning with our caregivers and family members. Your world, (your life) supports your ANGLE of it. Stated another way, your ANGLES created your yesterday and will create the rest of your tomorrows.

Do you think that Mark Cuban's ANGLE on being a Millionaire is the same as a professional Athlete's who became a millionaire for playing football or soccer? Of course not. Cuban's ANGLE on money, is that money is free flowing, abundant, and evergreen. He doesn't know "want" or "lack" of money as an ANGLE. We can tell by looking at his "reality" and how he shows up in the world.

Comparatively, 80% of NFL players are close to bankruptcy within 2 years of retirement.[3] Their ANGLE of money, may look something like-- money isn't evergreen; that it must be used while it's here-it or that it comes with heavy personal obligation to the "crew/posse", family members and friends, so there is a tremendous amount of pressure. Maybe their ANGLE is they have to share to be "true to where they came from"... as if there is such a thing. The 80% have a WHOLE story around what money is, and isn't, what it means, what is right, wrong, good, bad, the whole shebang; In the words of Biggie Smalls, "Mo Money Mo problems".

If the ANGLE is that money is a problem, the athlete, lottery winner, etc., will get rid of it (subconsciously), so it is no longer a "problem." Certainly, this is not conscious. The ANGLES show up as decisions, choices, judgments, conclusions, and stories, which are acted upon. I can say, that in all of Cuban's sound bites, I can't recall him ever saying the more money he made, the more problems he had.

How many times, have you heard of a millionaire athlete filing bankruptcy and re-establishing his financial empire? Certainly, you don't hear of this for lottery winners. The glaring distinction is the ANGLE from which they are operating.

Consider how ANGLES show up in love and romance.

Do you know someone, or are you that someone, that witnessed dysfunctional love between your parents? I am a "someone" for sure. My parents are married and have been for almost 50 years, and their relationship, SUCKED. Often, my father, who was a Minister referred to my mother, as "the albatross around his neck". Of course, this was only in the house; At every church function, he was the ever doting husband and man of God. Talk about an ANGLE??!! Can you imagine how confused I was?? There were all these "rules" about inside/ outside, love behavior, relationship, and manipulation? Oh, it's worth mentioning, that my mother, in response to being these "love rules" well, let's just say, she was so desperate for love that she resorted to maneuvering and manipulation as most people do to get it.

In the world of personal development and self-help, you often hear about limiting beliefs creating your reality and how they have to be "released". They also talk about infinite possibilities that come from releasing limiting beliefs in conjunction with *the Positives.*

ANGLES are more than mere limiting beliefs and 10 times more powerful in creating our reality. As I said, in the self-help world, we are taught that once we remove the limiting beliefs that we will then have the life of our dreams.

NEWSFLASH~ the whole limiting beliefs thing is just a myth. Oh, no need to feel embarrassed, I drank the Kool-Aid too at one point.

Consider this...

Limiting beliefs can be both negative and "positive", but are limitations just the same. Any limitation whether it is negative or positive is an ANGLE, because it restricts your actions, decisions and possibilities; they are like electric force fields or fences keeping the stuff you desire out, while at the same time, keeping the stuff YOU DON'T want in.

Remember, ANGLES are very defined points of view. If you believe that the only way to be successful, is to work 80 hours per week at a job you hate, to pay your dues, that is a limitation right? It forecloses the possibility of anything else, right? The flip side is that many people will applaud your work ethic. Yet, you know that you are exhausted and have little time for anything or anyone else.

Or, if you think, that "I am a good person", because I stayed married to someone who was unfaithful to me. I "stuck it out", many people would applaud the fact that you "hung in there", but how does this create possibility?

I am not saying you shouldn't hang in there, or stick it out with someone. What I am highlighting is that ANGLES can take on any character, "positive" or "negative" "good or bad". Anywhere there is a limitation, on who you can be, do, or have; it's because of an ANGLE. That ANGLE (point of view) dictates where you will go, who you will be, and what you will do. Limitation and possibility cannot exist in the same space. If you are limiting yourself with the ANGLE that you are a good person, to hang in there, even though you are unhappy, then leaving to be happy is not a possibility.

Interestingly, the ANGLE creates an either or situation that doesn't actually exists. It is not stay or go, as if you stay forever or go forever. What if, "it is just go for a little while"? Maybe, just making that an option will create the space for real change to take place?

Being a "good person", is an ANGLE, just as being a "bad person" is. If you make something "right", that is an ANGLE and even where that "rightness" does not serve your truth, and you are killing yourself to be "right", that will create your reality.

Are you someone or have you ever heard someone speak of "paying their dues". Perhaps you have been entrained to believe that all of the goodness and abundance you want to experience in your life has to be "earned". What doesn't kill you makes you stronger and all that jazz. Do you know what I am talking about? Being happy, wealthy, and having the world at your fingertips without suffering, would just be, well, "wrong"... right?

It's an ANGLE, that you have to suffer and that only when you have "suffered enough", you've earned the right to what is already yours, by virtue of your Divinity- the right to all of the yumminess life has to offer.

Ask yourself, whether there is something you think you need to do, accomplish or overcome to feel worthy of the life you want? Perhaps you think you need to lose 50 pounds, before you find love, or take your gifts out into the world; that is an ANGLE. It is limiting you from having the love you want, right now, just as you are. What if it's possible to have the love right now, without losing 50 pounds, or 2 years of therapy- what would happen if you deleted, unlocked, unplugged, removed, and devalued, the ANGLE? Is it possible, that you could be deserving and worthy, right now, just as you are?

Now, some of you may say, yes, Tiphanie, but some things need to be "judged". Everywhere you are judging anything; you are locking that judgment into place in your life and limiting your life. With every limitation, your life and your living become that much smaller, and your life and living becomes less and less about you.

The good news is that we can choose which ANGLES we take and thereby create our reality. YAY! Even better news is that choosing which ANGLES we take, does not require years of therapy, deep diving into the past or reliving traumas. It is simply becoming fully aware- more on that to come as well.

ANGLES of Influence- The AOI

Did you know that 97% of your thoughts, feelings and beliefs are not your own?

You would agree that babies are born ANGLE-LESS, right? They have no points of view, judgments, conclusions or opinions- they are just pure true self...

Most people are other people. Their thoughts are someone else's opinions, their lives a mimicry, their passions a quotation. Oscar Wilde

As babies, we are born whole and perfect. Neither you nor I, were born with judgments and conclusions about how life "should" operate. Babies are **ANGLE-LESS**, a bottle and a clean pamper is a good time for a baby.

Being born "ANGLE-LESS", begs the question, "if the Angles aren't yours, then whose are they?" Many of them belong to your AOI-i.e. ANGLES that you have resisted or reacted to and/or aligned or agreed with; either unconsciously or consciously.

Some ANGLES may just be that energy that you are experiencing from random people who just happen to be vibrating at a particular level. *What if* the vast majority of your thoughts, beliefs, conclusions, assumptions, computations, and judgments (ANGLES) that you are living, acting and making choices from were not actually your ANGLES but just "stuff you were picking up on around you?

As children we watched our parent's relationships, or the lack of relationship and we "buy" their ANGLES. [By "buy" I mean totally, in alignment and agreement with]. We "buy" their ANGLES about how to love and be in relationship with another person. Of course as children, we are not necessarily making a conscious choice to "buy" a particular ANGLE but rather, align with it, to belong, connect, or survive in that environment.

To illustrate how this could potentially show up, let's say, after years of witnessing, some level of love dysfunction, your parents finally divorce. You choose to live with your mother, who proceeds to trash and bash not only your father, but all men. In fact, she goes so far as to say, that there is NO SUCH THING AS UNCONDITIONAL LOVE. Again, you align, agree with and/or buy this ANGLE as your own. If you are a boy, then you see yourself as bad, because ALL men are bad and if you are a woman something interesting happens. On the one hand, you long for loving companionship, you long to be accepted and wanted just as you are. On the other, your allegiance to your mother and conclusion that she is "right" leads you to see men as the enemy. Further, that there is no such thing as unconditional love; correspondingly, you will buy the ANGLE that no one will love you for who and what you are unconditionally. Also, you begin to question, your mother's love, since she has specifically said, that there is no such thing as unconditional love, but says she loves you. All of these ANGLES are driving your choices, decisions, and actions.

An internal struggle begins when you align and agree or resist and react with a particular ANGLE. What you desire i.e. your truth and your ANGLE are in conflict.

Are you that someone that continues to struggle with one bad relationship after another, or are a participant in a series of non-committal unfulfilling relationships, or unhappily alone?

Do you find yourself maneuvering and manipulating, to get your mate, partner, date, spouse, to do, be or act the way that you want or need them to?

There is no judgment or "wrongness" here this is just to shed light on the power of ANGLES. The thing is, by manipulating and maneuvering, you are operating from an ANGLE.

Ultimately, on some level you either recreate the same relationship your parents had, or seek to avoid it. That "avoidance" leads to emotional separation because it is based on the "wrongness" of the other person; More on "wrongness" later.

An illustration closer to home would be my losses of the babies and struggle with fertility. Do you think someone who has successfully had children almost on demand, then miscarries would have the same ANGLE as someone who is actively trying to conceive, gets pregnant and then miscarries? Of course not. I can assure you, despite the other more obvious differences, Michelle Duggar's (the mom with 19 kids) ANGLES on miscarriages and successful pregnancy is markedly different from my own.

Whether you come from an awesomely loving family, or a family like mine, that puts the "dys" in dysfunctional, you are bringing, creating or attracting things into your life, based upon the ANGLES of others. How many conclusions, decisions, and rationalizations have you come to in your life based on someone else's ANGLES (i.e. those things you have been engrained, entrained and told to belief)?

For example, if you grew up in an environment, where poverty was considered "noble" and brought you closer to God. Your ANGLE, would be that money and God were not in alignment, and thus, your decisions would bring you closer to God; but push money- consciously and/or unconsciously, out of your life. Essentially, you are buying the ANGLE, that prosperity and loving God are diametrically opposed. Your AOI (Angles of Influence) would reinforce that belief through their realities. For example, they would be deeply religious, but always struggling to make ends meet, or living with "just enough" financially. Maybe your AOI judge those with money. Perhaps they refuse to receive things that have high monetary value, labeling it is being greedy or pride. In those instances, certainly, a relationship with God would be present, but a relationship or having money would be almost non-existent; or as soon as money comes in, it's gone.

Another illustration would be, if you grew up as I did with lack and the belief that God favors some people more than others. Your ANGLE would be that some people are better in the eyes of God than you. Intellectually, you know this isn't true. You may even find scripture or other spiritual text that would support that this isn't rational thinking, but your ANGLE, that you are less than- lingers and guides your decisions and actions.

Correspondingly, your reality will be created based on this ANGLE that God likes other people more than you. In this illustration, perhaps you are constantly struggling to be a different person, or more like "that person" that God likes more, that God will be pleased with you and give you the desires of your heart. That ANGLE of less than, has you putting everyone else's needs above your own, to your financial, emotional, spiritual detriment so that you will be seen as worthy of God's favor; a sort of quid pro quo with God. The ANGLE may show up in the form of indecision, as you "wait on God to bless you", rather than taking decisive action to do something that would make you happy. It could show up as you stopping short of the finish line (your goal), because, "everyone knows, only people "like them" (i.e the people God favors more than you), ever win.

Another ANGLE of how God and financial blessings would be, the belief, that if you are in service to yours, you shouldn't profit. For example, if you are a healer, spiritual teacher, a life coach, or some other profession where you contribute to the betterment of the lives of others, the ANGLE may be… that since those are your God given gifts, you should do them for free; that you would be "wrong" to be financially compensated to improve people's lives.

Similarly, an ANGLE could be, that if you are using a gift and something is easy for you, it is your duty as a God-fearing person, to giveaway your gifts for free.

Some of you may be thinking, "Well, Tiphanie, what's wrong with that, I want my AOI to be proud and pleased with me?" The question is, "Are you proud of you?" If you have to suppress who you are, to garner someone's love and admiration, is it you they are loving? Do you want to live your entire life in a mask? Your very point of existing, is self-expression and to be the gift and contribution that your truth is to the world.

The aim of life is to live, and to live means to be aware, joyously, drunkenly, serenely, divinely aware. Henry Miller

ANGLES can also show up, as not valuing your truth and elevating the truths of others above your own. As I discuss later in the book, gathering data is one thing, but elevating that data to truth, above your own may prove devastating to you in many ways. For me, it was the loss of babies. For you, it may be lost money, opportunities, love, passion, happiness.

"Every time you don't follow your inner guidance, you feel a loss of energy,

loss of power, a sense of spiritual deadness."
Shakti Gawain

Now, for those of you, who say, "No way, am I like my AOI, I am not living from their point of view".
Check this out.

We would like to think, that we are nothing like our less than "ideal" AOI and in many ways that may be true. HOWEVER, if you are making conscious decisions, based upon a desire or promise to yourself, to never be like them, you are still creating your life from the ANGLES of Influence. You are living a life, not based on your personal truth, but rather, a desire to not live their truth.

While many of your ANGLES are directly tied to your family, friends and peers, still, others may just be the energy that you are experiencing from random people who just happen to be vibrating at a particular energetic frequency. In other words, it just may be your awareness of your surroundings.

Have you ever stopped at a red traffic signal, suddenly you begin feeling irritated even though nothing was wrong- you weren't running late and were probably in good spirits when you got in the car? It is possible that you may be picking up on someone else's energy (not your own) who is under the strain of running late, and whose day began with stress and strain?

Let me explain...

ANGLES - ENERGY & RESONANCE

Have you ever said, or heard someone talk about "Good Vibes"? I know that the Beach Boys made a fortune on the song, "Good Vibrations." When you are aware of your vibration, you generally refer to them as "feelings" and/or emotions. Emotions are said to be energy + motion.

When you are aware of energetic vibrations in your consciousness, (thinking part of the mind), you call them feelings. Have you ever noticed, that you can pick up on how someone else is feeling? What you are tuning into in those moments is that person's energetic vibrations. Your vibrations are what you send out into the world. How many times, have you walked into a room, office, church, or crowd of people (etc.), where there was previously tension, and you "sensed the energy of tension"?

How many times, have you heard the phrase, "the tension was so thick, you could cut it with a knife"? In those cases and countless others, the energy that was or remained in the room, was from those that previously and still occupied it. You were merely "picking up on it".

A more common illustration is when you have a feeling or was thinking about someone; the phone rings, and it is that person or they show up at your door. These are examples of you sending energy or vibrations out, and matching then marrying someone else's energetic vibration.

Similarly, have you ever gone into a doctor's office or business, and immediately upon entering you felt "good vibes" or even bad vibes? A home can become filled with anger or love and comfort, and though the regular occupants may not be aware of the energy or vibration, (the good or bad vibes,) a visitor will immediately feel or notice the energy.

Given that we are both receivers and transmitters of energy, we pick up on the AOI as well, as the society as a whole. Energy is everywhere, it cannot be destroyed or created, it simply changes form.

This is how, as a stranger, you can see someone you have never met, and get an "eerie feeling" or "good vibe".

Has this ever happened to you? Your day starts great, and then all of a sudden, you are irritated or pissed off.... Nothing has changed or triggered it; you are just pissed off and becoming increasingly agitated. Or maybe, you have walked into a room and noticed "tension". No one has said anything, but you can just since the tension in the air...?

See, that's because, each of us, is a sort of energetic satellite a sort of sponge...

Science tells us, that EVERYTHING is energy, including thoughts, feelings, etc. So as an energetic sponge you are capable of picking up the vibes of other people's feelings, thoughts, and beliefs every day. As you move about your day, you are soaking up other people's "vibes" and because you haven't been taught to know which ones are yours and which are other peoples- you think those thoughts, beliefs are yours, and then act, because you think it's yours.

A VERY VERY VERY Quick Science Lesson:

This idea of everything is energy is not new. Albert Einstein, turned the scientific community upside down over 100 years ago, when he definitively proved his theory of relativity. The theory of relativity goes a little something like this, $e = mc^2$. According to Einstein, mass and energy are equivalent. An object's mass is a form of energy, and energy is a form of mass. It could be said, that this theory was the birth of quantum theory and physics.

Scientists, and more specifically, Quantum Physicists have shown that, while matter appears visibly to be solid, when examined under a high powered microscope and broken down to its smallest measurable components, called quanta, i.e. Atoms, neutrons, electrons, and molecules, all matter is mostly empty space intermingled with Energy.

Science tells us that if we took a drop of blood or a layer of skin, and placed it under a microscope, the cells of the skin and blood would be visibly vibrating. Similarly, if you placed a piece of paper under a high powered microscope, you would see the atoms and molecules of the paper vibrating.

Energy cannot be created or destroyed it simply changes shape and form. It is constantly vibrating and moving in waves called frequencies. While energy is in constant movement, it vibrates at various frequencies ranging from extreme high to extreme low on different wavelengths. Think water. Water can become steam, snow, ice, mist, but it is still water.

Like energy waves or vibrations attract like energy waves, hence the term, "Like ATTRACTS Like"- Ever heard of the phrase, "on the same wavelength?"

As you move about your day, every second, you are sending out energetic vibrations which are resonating, with similar vibrations. You are in many ways, a radar or radio, sending and receiving based on a specific frequency, which is being downloaded by your subconscious and conscious minds. The information is being received by you and everyone else on the planet, via energetic vibrations. You are simultaneously, receiving and translating the energetic vibrations of everyone and everything around you, in various forms, such as feelings, intuition, etc.

THOUGHTS AS ENERGETIC IMPULSES

As previously noted, EVERYTHING, in the Universe, including our bodies, and more specifically, our **thoughts are energy**. Each and every one of our thoughts is an energetic impulse. The thoughts (energetic impulses) we hold in our heads are as real as the things that we hold in our hands, see with our eyes, hear with our ears and smell with our noses.

All of the physical things we can sense with our five senses once began as thoughts. For example, when Henry Ford conceived the first car, he held a clear detailed image of the automobile in his mind before he began building it; it couldn't be built without the thought that it was possible.

Thoughts are things.

My favorite example of thoughts becoming things is the great inventor Nikola Tesla. Among Tesla's numerous inventions were

the modern radio, fluorescent lighting, the Tesla induction motor, the Tesla coil, the alternating current (AC) electrical supply system that included a motor and transformer, and 3-phase electricity.[4] Tesla stated:

"Before I put a sketch on paper, the whole idea is worked out mentally. In my mind, I change the construction, make improvements, and even operate the device. Without ever having drawn a sketch I can give the measurements of all parts to workmen, and when completed all these parts will fit, just as certainly as though I had made the actual drawings. It is immaterial to me whether I run my machine in my mind or test it in my shop. The inventions I have conceived in this way have always worked. In thirty years there has not been a single exception. My first electric motor, the vacuum wireless light, my turbine engine and many other devices have all been developed in exactly this way."

When we think or feel, we send out a fine celestial substance that is as real as the light, electricity, and heat vibrations; and while these celestial substances are not readily evident to our five senses, they exist just the same. I realize the tendency of many of us, (I was born in the "Show Me State"), is to disbelieve what we cannot experience with our five (5) senses.

I invite you to think in these terms, a large magnet's ability to magnetize steel is not evident to our five senses, yet the power of the magnetic vibrational force is very real. There are sound waves of which no human ear can hear, yet they exist just the same.

There are varying degrees of vibrational frequencies between the highest and lowest frequencies. When you are vibrating on a higher level energetic frequency, your experience includes feelings of eagerness, expansive, buoyance, happiness, cheerfulness, passion, bright, lightness and hopefulness. Accordingly, you will emit similar energy that will impact and influence others who are receptive to those higher level vibrations, to cooperate with and/or follow your lead.

Comparatively, when you are in or vibrating on the lower level frequencies, you feel depressed, weak, hopeless, dense, worried, fearful and "stuck". Unlike the higher level frequencies, you will tend to be led rather than leading others.

ANGLES are kinks, chains, blocks in the flow of energy. They restrict or prevent you from harnessing the power of your truth and receiving the things you desire. They are energetic plugs locked into place by our judgments, conclusions, beliefs, opinions and the like.

Understanding, how ANGLES and energy are intertwined, enables each of us to use the energetic vibrations of our thoughts to our benefit, just as we do with light, electricity and other forms of energy.

I would even go so far to say, that how it all "works", isn't terribly important. After all, for hundreds of thousands of years, people, didn't understand or know "how" the sun worked as a thermonuclear reactor, but it didn't stop them from using it's to sustain life, travel, stay warm, and grow crops.

The general thoughts of each of us will determine the vibrational frequency we receive from others. We can only receive those thoughts that are in RESONANCE and HARMONY with the general thoughts we hold ourselves. Illustrating this point of vibrational thought frequency, William Atkinson author of *Thought Vibration*, states, "Many of the "stray thoughts" which come to us are but reflections or answering vibrations to some strong thought sent out by another." Our minds are receiving these thoughts and believing them to be our own, because we are vibrating on the same or similar frequency to receive it.

If you are feeling a little melancholy, you are more likely to pick up on the energy and frequency of those who are also melancholy and/or more melancholy than you, because you are at that vibrational frequency.

When you send out a thought, you will only receive back thoughts that are in vibrational harmony with it. To illustrate this point, look at your thought as an instrument. If you have two guitars, if you play the C string, the other guitar will also play a C note; it won't play a G or F, but a C. Whatever "*key*", or energetic vibration you send out, it will be returned to you.

Remember like vibrational frequencies attract like vibrational frequencies; as noted by Atkinson,

> *"Just as a note of the violin will cause the thin glass to vibrate and "sing", so will a strong thought tend to awaken similar vibrations in minds attuned to receive it. ... If we are thinking high and great thoughts, ours minds acquire a certain keynote corresponding to the character of the thoughts we have been thinking. And this keynote, once established- we will be apt to catch the vibrations of other minds keyed to the same thought."*

Thankfully, you can change your vibrational frequency instantly, any time you wish. Skeptical? Trust me, it really is quite easy.

Here, I will show you. Close your eyes and picture yourself on a beautiful beach, with crystal blue water, and beautiful sand. You can smell the sea air, it isn't too hot, and there is just a slight breeze from the ocean waves breaking… hmmmmm… doesn't that feel wonderful? Yes, it is really, that easy...Told you, you could shift your vibration at any time.

Understanding emotions (emotion + motion) vibrations is important because none of us is an island. We share and crave to have experiences with others. However, given that we are both receivers and transmitters of energy, if we are not aware of the ANGLES "floating" around we could end up stuck, unhappy, possibly broke and feeling hopelessly locked behind a glass wall watching others feast off the joys of life, while we sit back with only the indigestion. Here is the rub- the emotional junk that's holding us back wouldn't even be our stuff! I say, if I am going doing, at least let it be by my OWN stuff… Are you with me?

Check this out…

You do not need to know the specific situation, circumstance, occurrence, relationship, or origin of the ANGLE. We are not trying to "get in touch with the wounded inner child, or heal trauma by reliving it". In fact, the more you don't go into the details, and just note the energy around the ANGLE, the easier it will be to shift and clear it. I just want you to go to the heart of the universe, which is Energy.

If you begin to find yourself oddly resentful, or procrastinating, feeling guilty, or unmotivated, or gripped with fear though nothing has changed in your environment, ask yourself, "whose is this, where did that come from or who does that belong to?" Just ask the question, DON'T LOOK FOR THE ANSWER! Notice, how you feel as you ask yourself the question.

ANGLES of Creation Decoded

Our ANGLE(s) create our reality, not the other way around. The result of the ANGLE can be seen by way of what *is* or *is not* showing up in your lives and in your conscious decisions. Though ANGLES show themselves in the thinking part of the mind (conscious), they are rooted in our subconscious minds, handed down through the generations, programmed via our AOI- locked in place throughout judgments, conclusions, assumptions and beliefs. More on how the ANGLES get locked in place to follow.

This is not to judge any ANGLE as good or bad, positive or negative, rather, I am saying that your ANGLES that are not your own, are the only things powerful enough to stand between you, and the life that you desire and deserve. No one can give you-you, but YOU; the YOU that you are, stripped naked of judgments, conclusions, opinions, conditions, beliefs and other "True Self" hindering belief systems.

Any and every where you are functioning and acting from a pre-defined ANGLE, about how the world is or is not working, what is or is not possible in your life, you cannot see or become aware of anything that is not a match for that ANGLE.

Today, your life is the sum total of all of your ANGLES, conclusions, solutions, answers, and other AOI. It is vital to becoming a Radical Self-Expert, that you be able to identify which ANGLES you are operating from and clear them in order for you to have, do, and be, what is uniquely designed just for you.

Our ANGLES are locked in place in the subconscious mind by our judgments, answers, conclusions, assumptions, and the like. Think of your ANGLES as an obstruction or electric doggy fence. Your ANGLES do not allow you to move in any direction, no matter how desperately you may desire to.

Here is another interesting tidbit about ANGLES.

Not only are ANGLES limiting, but they can sometimes be so innocuous, we don't even recognize that we "bought" they ANGLE as our own.

Here Are Some Common Angles- Do Any of These *Feel* Familiar?

Ever hear any of these growing up...

"Life is hard" and they should "prepare for the worst but hope for the best"

"Don't get your hopes up; you don't want to be disappointed when it doesn't work out".

"You can't have everything, just be grateful for what you have before you lose that too".

Ever hear, "we can't afford it... you can't have your cake and eat in too."

Or how about, "we don't have any extra because you kids just keep needing things..."

Perhaps, "I had to give up my dreams, to raise you."

"Money is the root of all evil."

"Money changes people for the worst".

"You can't be wealthy and serve God."

"If it looks too good to be true, it probably is."

"You can't make money doing that."

"Why start a business when you have a good job?"

"Who would pay you to do that?"

"We aren't made out of money."

"She's a doctor, but you know, you aren't as smart as she is..."

"I just have a fear of success."

Any of those sound familiar? Check this out... if you think that money is the root of all evil, or that having money would mean that you would lose friends, or people would only want you for money, then you will constantly push away, opportunities where you could receive money.

ANGLES Run Deep – One Brain 2 Minds~ Conscious and Subconscious Minds

> *"Although we all have one brain, we possess two minds or two phases of mind power - CONSCIOUS and SUBCONSCIOUS. It is important to understand the function of the CONSCIOUS MIND and the SUBCONSCIOUS MIND, because each one has different functions, abilities and capacities. Dr. Robert Anthony*

For clarity and better perspective, I believe a brief explanation of the conscious and subconscious minds is in order here. The conscious mind is that part of your mind that is responsible for reasoning and logic.

Picture a car. It is often said, that the conscious mind is like the steering wheel. Comparatively, the subconscious mind which determines attitudes, beliefs, how you perceive yourself and others, your values and motivations is EVERY OTHER PART OF THE CAR. The subconscious mind is developed via life experiences, beliefs handed down from our parents and environments, etc. Dr. Bruce Lipton has termed the subconscious mind a "tape player."[5] There is no reasoning or understanding in the subconscious mind, it merely records information.

Dr. Lipton has concluded that the subconscious mind, is strictly a playback machine with preprogrammed behaviors.

Think of things this way- have you ever logically known something and did the opposite? In those moments, your actions were not guided by reason and/or logic, but rather, a feeling, a thought, something you were programmed to do because of your upbringing, experiences, beliefs, etc.—the subconscious mind.

The subconscious mind occupies 96-99% of your mental real estate. If I owned 96% of the city, and you 4%, who would run the city? I would! Simple enough to understand, right? It is the same for the subconscious mind and the conscious mind.

Even if the conscious mind is operating at optimal speed and maximum capacity, it is still at best, only 4% of your mental real estate; this is why no amount of positive thinking without the enrollment or some form subconscious mind bypass will work to achieve permanent lasting results. Essentially, you are trying to trick your energy, and since you are the energy, you know it a half-truth at best, and a bold faced lie at its most honest.

Your subconscious mind is the vault of memories and where the conscious mind and subconscious mind are in conflict, the subconscious mind will mop the floor with the conscious mind.

Here is the challenge when it comes to the mind, both conscious and subconscious. It cannot and does not process "negatives". Meaning, when you tell yourself not to think about something, it has to think about that thing to be "right"- get it?? If I say, don't think about a sunflower. What came to mind? A sunflower, right?

Our subconscious minds have no sense of humor, play no jokes and cannot tell the difference between reality and an imagined thought or image. What we continually think about eventually will manifest in our lives." Robert Collier

How do you fix this? By getting your subconscious mind to cooperate with the conscious mind, i.e. clearing you're your judgments, conclusions, limiting beliefs and other ANGLES. Operate in conjunction with you, not in opposition of you; Or, by bypassing it as much as possible.

One of the cool things about being a Self-Expert is you don't need to relive all the trauma, drama and pain in your life. Or even know where or from whom you bought the ANGLE. The particulars of the ANGLE are not as relevant, as to the energy (feelings) that the ANGLE brings up for you. You don't need to specifically identify the ANGLE either. Whether it is upset, sadness, anger, guilt, whatever it is, do not spend hours, days or years on trying to identify the specific emotion.

You just need to become aware of the energy of the ANGLE. I will discuss in depth how and why the energy of the ANGLE is more important than labeling the ANGLE itself.

Many of you may be thinking, if the ANGLES are/can be secret, unseen, or unheard, how do you access them? Right on, another champion question. You are on it, dog gon' it!

Remember, I told you that an Affirmation put to proper use, would be effective? Well, they are great ANGLE crackers. It is so easy to do, and by doing this action step, you will see, *WHY* affirmations by themselves are ineffective for creating permanent and lasting change.

ACTION STEP Part I.

I invite you to reverse engineer your life right now.

If you do not have the results in a particular area of your life, ask yourself, "What ANGLES, would I have to have, that would create this situation I am in now?"

Refer back to some of the ANGLES above, and see what comes up for you. Note the energy around what you want. If you find that as quickly as you make money, you are broke just as fast, that is an ANGLE.

Certainly, ANGLES are much deeper than those examples, because they are unique to you. Further, there are layers on upon layers of locked energy from our AOI in our lineage. The examples, are more to give you a place to start. Below, I give you a very effective technique for unlocking your ANGLES. Once you know what your ANGLES are, you will be able to apply your Detector of Truth and KNOW if the ANGLE is yours or not so you can flush them out of your system with the DE-WAY. More on the Detector of Truth and the DE-WAY in the "D" Step of RADICAL.

ACTION STEP PART II.

Draw three columns on a sheet of paper.

Now, write down 5 things for which you would like to have, be or do. For example, a loving relationship or more money, you would write that down on the left side of the paper.

In the middle section (column 2) write down a positive affirmation of the thing you want to have, do, or be.

After you write the affirmation, IMMEDIATELY without THINKING write down the first thing that comes to your mind following the affirmation in the third column on the right. So for example, if you write, I am deserving of love, write down what your "mind" says to you after you write that down.

I only asked you to do that or five things, but you can do this exercise for everything in your life, that you don't have, but want to have do or be.

Desire	Affirmation	Feeling About Affirmation
. love	I am lovable	If I was lovable, my ex wouldn't have cheated on me.

**Also as you write down the thoughts immediately following the affirmation, note the VOICE of the thought that is concluding, judging or limiting you.

For example, if you have the point of view that money is evil, whose voice do you hear attached to that judgment? Do you hear your pastor or priest? Perhaps your parents, grandparents, sisters?

Note all of these things because they are all relevant to your point of view, awareness and truth

ACTION STEP: PART III- Who Does That Belong To?

For the next 5 days, when you have a thought, belief, judgment, pain in your body, limitation, upset, feeling or anything else.

Ask yourself, "Where did that come from? Who does that belong to?" You do not need to figure out where it came from, or who's thought/belief/feeling, it is- you just need to ask the question.

Do this for everything, for 5 days straight. Note what happens when you ask the questions. DO NOT ANSWER the questions, just ASK them.

Some of those thoughts may be "good" some "bad", ask the questions anyway; Whether the thought/belief/feeling/ limitation is good, bad, right or wrong, hot or cold, whatever.

Ask the questions.

If You've Made it This Far, YAY! Now, Let's Tie This Step Together, Cool?

Remember I said, that your ANGLES create your reality. They act as almost a prism with which you experience the world. Any place in your life, where, you are operating from ANGLES rather than your unique truth, you are bringing those people, places and things into your reality; this includes all of your limiting ANGLES and potentially all of those limiting ANGLES from your AOI. YIKES!

So if you are currently believing, trusting and choosing the ANGLES of your family, friends, abusers, community, or other external things, you will attract and experience those things that are in alignment with your ANGLES

If your ANGLE is lack and poverty, guess what you will experience. This can be so very painful as I am sure you know, because everything within you, is saying, there is something more for you. It is downright spirit crushing, to live in a space of incongruence, where what you desire within you, is not what you are experiencing outside of you.

The effects of buying or living through your AOI, is multi-faceted:

(1) You deny what is true for you and as James Allen pointed out, happiness can only come when your inner and outer self are aligned.

(2) You begin to see that something is "wrong" with you because you are not like your family.

(3) You feel unhealthily different because uniqueness is not praised the way uniformity is.

(4) You suppress more and more of your truth, losing more and more of you.

(5) YOU CAN ONLY RECEIVE the frequency of your AOI, because you are only open to receiving their frequency. Your ANGLES are keeping you locked inside of the space of impossibility. Your ANGLES do not permit you to experience the joy of who you are. Consequently, you feel unfulfilled, empty, resentful, and angry.

(6) As a result of you vibrating on the lower frequencies of discontent, resentment, anger, guilt, blame, etc., you have unexplained health problems, difficulty being in relationships, low self- esteem.

Simple, right? If you are one energetic vibrational frequency, you can only receive the experiences of that frequency. Can you experience joy and rage at the exact same moment? Of course not. Can you experience possibility and contraction at the same time? Certainly not. Why do we always try to make a baby that is crying laugh? You want the baby to laugh so they will STOP crying. Two energies, emotions, feelings that are polar opposites can't exist in the same space.

Gemma's Story

A real life illustration is my client, who we will call Gemma. Gemma grew up in an uneducated, not particularly loving home, were lack, scarcity and not complaining was a way of life. The only way to get ahead, was hard-work and sacrifice. Anything other than the basics of food, water and shelter, were of the devil and "un-Godly excess".

Even after meeting and marrying a wonderful man, they would never buy more than they needed, take a vacation, and though they "worked hard" they continued to struggle with lack and scarcity just as her parents (and her parents' parents did).

They didn't even go on a honeymoon. Their belief was that poor people didn't go on honeymoons, and that they needed to save everything they had, because it wasn't much and you didn't know when or if you were going to get more; they believed that the worst was coming, so they had to prepare for it.

Suffice it to say, that their reality looked exactly like those ANGLES. It was a vicious cycle for them, as they read the self-help books (at the library); they would never waste money on buying books. They were chronically unhappy, tired, overworked, and were buckling under the weight of it all. They felt extreme guilt for wanting more than what they had and not wanting to struggle financially anymore. Fun was almost non-existent, as every penny was stored away "just in case". Their vibrational frequency was dialed into lack, poverty, guilt and scarcity; unsurprisingly, their reality was lack, poverty, guilt and scarcity.

Desperate she contacted me via personal message on one of the social media sites and we began working together on her ANGLES. After doing the exact exercises I am sharing with you in this book, she cracked her ANGLES, and understood, that just because she was from her family, she was NOT her family. She used her Detector of Truth and realized, that those ideas of not receiving good things, and more than she "needed" were not hers. Though, intellectually, she knew that there had to be something more, her ANGLES were creating the life of her family.

Together we cleared those points of views via the exact techniques I am sharing with you in this book. Within one week (7 days), her life became hers!

I feel so honored to share with you, that she is in a job that loves with an awesome salary, takes regular vacations, and has committed to being a Radical Self-Expert. She has tools to "guard" her vibration and chooses those vibrational frequencies that are in alignment with her truth.

ANGLES of FEAR & JUDGMENT

Generally, the most common ANGLES are related to fear and judgment. I call these two ENERGY TROLLS, because they just suck the life out of everything, UGH!

Fear and Judgment are so insidious because they are the parents to all the other ANGLES. Unchecked they are like predators that feed on every aspect of your life- devouring everything and leaving only carnage in their wake. The effects are devastating, ranging from complete paralysis, to self-loathing and anger.

The Energy Troll of Fear...

First and foremost, fear creates an immediate contraction and shrinking effect on you. It creates a heaviness in your spirit and limits all possibilities. Fear prevents you from naming and claiming what is rightly yours as a Divine and Infinite Being. It stifles your creativity and persuades you to stay small and not step into the magic that is your truth.

It triggers the fight or flight response, which rarely contributes to creating the life of your dreams. Fear encourages you to stop short of your desires, rather than taking that final step.

The Fear Energy Troll spawns worry and doubt... so powerful is this troll that it has you creating your future from events that have not even happened yet. Entire treatises have been written on the devastating and destructive Energy Troll of Fear. Worry not; you can shift the energy of fear with your De-WAY and Detector of Truth.

The Energy Troll of Judgments

"Doubt yourself and you doubt everything you see. Judge yourself and you see judges everywhere. But if you listen to the sound of your own voice, you can rise above doubt and judgment. And you can see forever." Nancy Lopez

Judgments in particular are quite tricky ANGLES. Along with their partner in emotional crime, fear, judgments are tricky indeed. Not only do we use them to make sense of the world, we have categorized them in terms of "good and bad", positive or negative. Judgments, any judgment creates a limitation on what we can have, be, or do.

The funny thing is, we think that by judging something, it will create the change in our behavior, circumstance or situation. When has that ever worked long-term? Whatever we judge someone else or something, we cement that judgment and keep ourselves stuck.

Remember, the subconscious mind doesn't see or understand negatives, it just reads commands like a computer. So when you are throwing your disdain about something in your life, or how someone is behaving, you are locking that in place for them and for you.

Think about something you have wanted to change in your life? Let's say, you have judged yourself as being a failure because you have not made a certain amount of money. Has that judgment put more money in your bank account? Or do you find that you continue to struggle? What about with your weight or health? Have you judged that your body as it is today is not acceptable? How has that worked out for you? The list of judgments we have about ourselves is unfortunately endless. How do all of those judgments feel by the way? When you judge yourself as bad or broke, or needing to do something other than be who you are—how does that feel? Heavy, light? Do those judgments make you want to venture out into the world and share your gifts? Or do they make you want to run and hide? Never fully showing up for your life or standing in your power, for fear of being "found out" as being less than perfect?

As we attempt to make sense of the world, by categorizing, concluding and judging, we tend to forget that how we judge others, is how we are ultimately judging ourselves- or in my case, I judge myself much more harshly than I did others

Whether you are judging others, or yourself, your sole focus is on what you are not, instead of the truth of who you are. The funny thing is, judgment is merely a summary of other people's feelings, ideas, and beliefs, which you have been conditioned to believe as your own. Babies are not born with judgments, it is something they are engrained and entrained to believe.

Picture a 3 or 5 year old. They dance when they feel like dancing, and can be disciplined and turn around 5 minutes later and come for a hug and a kiss like nothing happened. They can receive everything, and reject nothing, because they are not limited by judgments.

As Dr. Wayne Dyer so eloquently points out, "*Judgments prevent us from seeing the good that lies beyond appearances.*"

Consider this, everything you judge creates greater separation from you and the thing, or person you want to have or be with. Think of a friend, you think isn't the brightest or the cutest, or a friend who appears to have the perfect life. Isn't there a part of you, (however small), that you keep away from her? Maybe you don't go to her, for advice, because she isn't "bright", but what if, despite that, she actually had some valuable information, on who you could talk to? Maybe you don't talk the "perfect friend" because you don't want to appear less then, but what if she could share her struggle of how she got to where she is.

Judgments are about fixed ideas and belief systems. Since, they are fixed, by nature; they prevent other possibilities from being. For every judgment you have, there is a decision that follows it, and locks whatever the judgment you have in place. You are stuck in the limiting trap of what's right and wrong, good or bad... so as long as you have a judgment, a decision based on that judgment you will have no choice.

So check this out... judgments are completely an outside job. Meaning, they are not about our unique truth, but about someone or something else outside of us

As I said, for every judgment, there is a decision that locks that judgment in place and creates the separation between us and the good stuff we want.

Think about it for a moment... the perception of what other people think or feel is creating a separation and limitation on your life. Does that even make sense?

Firstly, you can't even know what someone else thinks or feels with 100% accuracy. Second, they are just like you, picking up on other people's energy, all day every day, so it may not even be there's to begin with... and third, if you were on an island, by yourself, would you judge yourself? Would you go, "would you say to yourself, I am so rude, I am so fat, or stupid" Heck no, you wouldn't say anything of the kind.

When you begin to judge yourself or anyone else, take a moment, and ask yourself, "What am I not allowing myself to receive by having this judgment? Then ask, "What possibilities am I limiting with my judgment?

ACTION STEP

If you could begin today, right now with a clean slate, walk out of your life as it is now and erase everyone's memory of you, and you could re-create your life to include ANYTHING you want... what would that be??

Write out a day in the life of the new you.... No judgments, no right, wrongs, goods, bads, negative, positives, conclusions, computations, just what feels right for you...

SIDE NOTE

Here is an interesting side note on fear—definitely something I will invite everyone to explore later with me in a book, video, or something...

So check this out... fear is often a misunderstood energy. Excitement and fear are the same feelings physiologically, right? Take this scenario. Have you ever been in a serious situation where you should have been "afraid", but were totally calm? Most people talk about such an experience as being in slow motion, having super human strength, a sixth sense or guardian angel. In those serious and sometimes life-threatening situations, being "afraid" would be understandable, right? How can it be though, that if you were "afraid" you knew exactly what to do and remained calm, had a guardian angel or sixth sense? What if it wasn't actually fear but instead you were MORE AWARE? Let me explain...

Think about this, when a child gets ready to hop in the swimming pool for the first time, or on the first day of school, what does a parent say to the child, "Don't be afraid". Consider this—maybe that child wasn't afraid, but just excited but couldn't in her/his young mind, "label" that feeling or emotion. So, when the parent says to him/her "don't be afraid", she goes, "oh, its fear I am feeling".

Later, as she grows up, whenever there's a feeling, resembling that excitement, or an unknown situation or experience, she thinks, "I'm afraid". See??? She was entrained to have fear and be afraid when what she was experiencing excitement.

Excitement is by its nature an expansive energy; it's a BIG emotion. Big emotions, are bigger, than what our minds can compartmentalize because they are expansive for a reason, right? They are to clue us to what is possible, to signal to us, that there is MORE than what we can see with our eyes or touch with our hands to light the fire in us, right?

The rub is that later, whenever that feeling of expansion comes up, instead of just allowing the big energy to be there, we shut it down as fear and close all the possibilities of having, being or doing more. This is just one example of how excitement can be *mis-identified* and entrained to be fear.

So when you think of something you truly desire, do you feel big and expansive, like, “OMG”? Most likely, that is just excitement, not fear. What if what we think is fear, is just excitement, so much excitement, that we are energetically overwhelmed by it? Conversely, what if what we think is fear, was really, just “greater awareness” designed for our benefit, or internal angel, or sixth sense for those serious and/or life or death situations?
No matter what the label is, you will be able to distinguish fear from excitement with your detector of truth, so YAY!

Step 3. D="De-Way" & Detector of Truth

Your ANGLES are LITERALLY, locking and limiting your capacity to change the things that aren't working. They are also stopping you from moving to the next level of success (whatever that is for you)The energy is what fuels the ANGLE. So, the more deeply held an ANGLE, the more energetic power, the ANGLE has and the BIGGER the limitation it is in your life and living.

Fascinatingly, there are a plethora of energies, which create limitation for you. Vibrational frequencies run the gamut, even the lower level vibrations of anger, guilt, fear, worry, blame, all are different energetically; all of which create varying degrees and manifest different limitations in your life. Guilt is not the same as fear. Worry is not the same energetically as blame.

Similarly, happiness, contentment, optimism and passion all have different energetic frequencies. Fascinating, right? When you are in AWE of someone or something, it doesn't necessarily mean that you are happy or content, right? Nope, energetically they are all different.

Fear of not having money, is not the same as money is the root of all evil. Do you see what I mean?

Although it may come in various forms, the general techniques for dealing with unwanted emotions involve things like:

i) Some sort of deep diving into the past…
ii) Unearthing every emotion since birth…some sort of quasi-therapy methods to identify and understand the why, how, and what of EVERY single emotion…
iii) Healing the inner child…
iv) "Relive it and heal it" techniques…
v) And on and on…

I don't know about you, but well, I like instant energetic shifts. Believe me, I did the therapy thing, but as you know now, I was not working on my stuff, but my AOI's stuff.

Carmen's Story

In fact, here is an interesting story. I had a client, Carmen. She was in therapy for about a year and was complaining about how she didn't feel like she was getting much traction in her growth. So I casually mentioned that she try the techniques and methods I am sharing with you. For 5 days, I had her ASK for every emotion, belief, conclusion and judgment, "whose is this? Is this mine?"

Within 24 hours, she called me excitedly, saying, "Tiph, oh my gosh, what the fu*k??" I said, "What's wrong Carm?" She noticed that the stuff she thought was making her crazy (her words), was not her stuff. They were just ANGLES.

As soon as she asked the questions of the ANGLES, something happened. She said, "I don't know what hell happened, but that's what I am talking about!" Of course, I laughed and told her to keep going. Since she was having so much success with that tool, I offered her another one. Which is the one I am about to share with you. So, I told her, when there is an ANGLE and she can feel an emotional charge on the ANGLE, to then do something I termed, "The De-WAY". She was like, "what the F*&k is that? (She used an F- bomb)"

I explained to her, that ANGLES have an energetic vibration.

If she wanted to have an instant shift, for those ANGLES, that were unnecessarily creating limitations on her life, then this is a simple, guaranteed way to do it. Being who she is, she was all in

Want to immediately shift that "stuff" that is weighing on your life a ton of bricks? Maybe you want to release fear immediately? The DE-WAY, is a way to immediately shift the locked energy that is creating those ANGLES of limitation in your life

Remember emotion is energy + motion.

The DE-WAY is a sort of clearing process to unlock the energy, and crack the ANGLE, to create space for you to receive what you are asking for from the Universe/God/Mother Earth/Your Higher Self.

Using the DE-WAY allows you to powerfully go to the life's blood of the limitation- the energy... you know:

- Go to all of those places where you have created your reality based on the ANGLE...
- Any and everywhere you have hurt and destroyed yourself in attempts to hold that ANGLE in place & BEYOND To those places where you feel blocked but can't find the words or identify the block.

The DE-WAY is EASY, INSTANT and POWERFUL! It is a sort of energetic detox, clients call it an "energetic colonic". When you use the DE-WAY with a particular ANGLE, issue, belief, it literally flushes all of the negative energy charge from your body and space.

As you will learn more in "C" section, you are asking the Universe/God/Mother Earth, Higher Self, to "clean you out" energetically, and release the limiting ANGLE. The awesome part, is that you don't have to know where the ANGLE came from, who's ANGLE it is, what it is, how it got locked in the place.

In other words, you don't need to know the "Deets" (Details) of the energy, you just need to ask and be willing to release it. COOL, right??? YAY! The Universe/God/Source/Your Higher Self is all knowing, and knows exactly what the ANGLE is and where it was locked.'

Also, everything underneath the ANGLE, belief, emotion energetically is released and cleared, no matter where the ANGLE of limitation is.

It is also important that you use the DE-WAY, or some other form of energy shifting technique so that you can know your truth. Clearing the energy, will maximize your Detector of Truth, to absolutely know what is true for you; more on the Detector of Truth coming in just a bit.

Keep in mind, ANGLES of limitation can be both "positive and negative". As I indicated before, ANGLES are those things that we made right about something, or wrong about something. They include things we react and resist, agree and align with. Anywhere you have concluded, that this is the only way, or you can't see any way for something to show up the way you want it, there is an ANGLE of limitation. You don't need to know where it is, or what it is. We are going directly to the source, which is the energy. Think of this technique like the people hundreds of thousands of years ago thought about the sun. They weren't sure how the sun worked, but that didn't stop them from harnessing the sun's power to their benefit.

Now, The DE-WAY can do anything to you or for you. It only releases the energy or the emotional charge that is creating the limitation in your life. Oh, and it is a lot of fun too.

SO HERE WE GO:***The DE-WAY***

When something "comes up for you", meaning an emotion, feeling, or thought of limitation, say:

Whatever, wherever, whenever, and ALL that this is, everywhere that I created and destroyed myself from it, through all time, space and realities, I choose now to De-create it, De-Value and Delete It. Inhale in for 5, release for 5. At the end of the breath, say out loud, YAY ME, YAY ME, YAY ME!

Now depending on the circumstances, you may need or want to change the wording a bit, but the most important language is: Everything that is not allowing___________(fill in the blank for what you want), all that this is, through all time, space and realities, I choose to now De-create, De-Value and De-lete it. Breathe in and out for 5 and finish with YAY ME!

<u>The short version:</u>*** *is simply- Everything that is not allowing me to have ________(fill in the blank- it could be love, money, peace, passion, clarity) , I choose to De-create, Devalue and Delete. Remember to fill in the blank with the thing you want. It could be, something like, "Everything that is not allowing me to release this anger, or everything that is not allowing me to be happy, or everything that is not allowing me to receive clarity money, joy, peace of mind, sleep, release excess* *weight and so on.*

We will go into greater application of the DE-WAY, after I explain the ALL IMPORTANT Detector of Truth below.

Now you are probably thinking, huh? Let's breakdown what you are saying...

First let's look at the "De" prefix... quoting Random House Dictionary:

"De prefix has its origins in Latin loanwords used to form verbs that denote motion or conveyance down from, away or off; reversal or undoing of the effects of an action; extraction or removal of a thing; thoroughness or completeness of action"[6]

DE-CREATE

"For you are the creator of your own reality, and life can show up in no other way for you than the way in which you think it will." **Neale Donald Walsh**

As defined by Webster's Dictionary, to create is to cause to come into being; to evolve from one's imagination; to arrange; to bring about[7]

We are the sum total of our ANGLES. Good, bad, right, wrong, positive and negative, ALL of the ANGLES from which we experience and exist. Whether you are Christian, Hindu Buddhist, Agnostic or Atheist, the inescapable truth is that, our thoughts, beliefs, conclusions, judgments, become the things in our lives.

The awesome news, is that for all of those things are not working or serving our highest purpose and good, we can choose something else. Yes, it is as simple as making a choice. If you can create something you don't like with passion, you can de-create it and create something you do like with the same amount of passion. It is a choice of what you are choosing to focus on. The "trick", is that for some, while the mind is willing and a portion of you may have a deep desire, it is clouded by the residue of the ANGLES' energy.

So by De-creating, you are both acknowledging yourself as the Creator of your life, and making another choice. It is a declaration and command to the universe. You are summoning all of the energy around that particular thing that you created, and saying, that wherever it is, even in the most remote places of your mind, body, spirit, lineage, and 4 corners of the earth, past lives (if you believe in them), you choose as the Creator to DECREATE it NOW! How freakin' awesome is that? Yes, you are that powerful! You just have to ask the universe to do it and say it as done.

"De-creating" generates a new flow of expansive energy of possibility. Whatever it is that is creating the limitation for you, you reversing or undoing the effects that you created as a result of your ANGLE or damage that ANGLE came to be in your life. Everywhere that you have agreed or aligned with an ANGLE or reacted or resisted an ANGLE, you are now choosing as the Creator of those things, to de-create them.

DE-VALUE

Value, per Webster's, is defined as: the relative worth or importance the abstract concepts of what is right, desirable or worthwhile; to esteem; meaningful.

The DeValue prong of the DE-WAY is important as you want to reverse or extract any worth, meaning, desirability, or importance of what is right regarding that ANGLE of limitation or the ANGLE in general. Now, some of you are thinking, why would I have value in something that is limiting me? Oh BOY... Check this out....

Perhaps you have an ANGLE, that if you were successful, you would lose your friends. Or maybe you don't want other people to feel badly, because you are successful and they aren't. This ANGLE, keeps you small. You have limited the possibilities of your life based upon the fear that you may lose friends, or guilt about what would happen to other people. Interestingly, you have no control whatsoever over what happens to other people, because just as you are the Creator of your life, they too create theirs, but I digress.

So the ANGLE of not wanting your parents to feel wrong or bad, or become more than your friends, is limiting. The value to you of holding the ANGLE in place, though false, is that by living your life smaller than your desires, you keep friends and show your parents respect. Crazy, right? So as the energy around that comes up, you need to devalue it.

It is worth noting that ANGLES, don't just begin with you. What I mean is, an ANGLE has been passed through your lineage. I can't even tell you, how many crazy ANGLES, my parents have and continue to operate from. What I know though, is that they just bought them, and because they created their reality around them, they operate from them as if they were true. It is not about blame or making them wrong- it just is.

My responsibility is not to change their awareness or consciousness, but rather, be the creator of the only thing for which I can control, and that is me. Similarly, the ANGLES that you may have are multilayered, multi-dimensional and generational

However, the good news is, the De-Way can create an almost instantaneous shift, such that, by moving the energy, you can go to your Detector of Truth, and operate from your true self. (More on the detector of truth to follow, I promise). It is no coincidence that it rhymes with Freeway, because it is an energy shift superhighway! ;-)

By stating that you De-Value, whatever that energy is, and everything underneath it, you are releasing whatever that ANGLE means to you and all of the value that you were attaching to it.

Now this will blow your mind!

In 2010, a Dr. Ali Binazir, concluded, that "Pain and negative emotions activate the reward centers of the brains causing unconscious addiction to those negative emotions." He notes that pain and negative emotions light up the brain, activating the beta-endorphin[8] and dopamine[9] pathways, just as cocaine and another narcotics do. Consequently, people can easily become addicted to those emotions physiologically.[10]

According to Dr. Binazir, the dopamine pathway becomes activated when we go into survival mode. The chief stress hormone of Cortisol[11], mediates the release of dopamine. It follows then, according to Dr. Binazir that when you are stressed out or in survival mode, your brain releases dopamine. Beta-endorphin is a powerful analgesic aka painkiller. It is analogous to a runner's high, where you can just keep running (forever) and then as soon as you get home, you can barely move.

Evolutionarily speaking, this makes total sense. As Dr. Binazir notes if you were injured a million years ago, on the Nile River (he says Savannah), your survival demanded that you be distracted from the pain of your injury until you could return to a place of seeming safety. Today, as it relates to negative emotions, the chemicals are tapping into that ancient "survival mind". Negative emotions of guilt, self-pity and anger activate the beta-endorphin and dopamine pathways.

Did that blow your mind or what? So not only does the ANGLE have emotional or psychological value to you, it potentially has physiologically value. Now you can see, why you must DE-VALUE, the ANGLE, the energy, through all time, places, dimensions, realities, and lineage.[12]

ACTION STEP:

For everything in your life that you would like to change, ask this question: "What is the value of me holding on to this ANGLE?" Just sit with that question, don't rush to answer it.

De-Lete

The word de-lete is from the Latin, delere which is to wipe out or destroy. By definition it means to eliminate especially by blotting out, cutting out or erasing.[13]

By "deleting" all of the energetic limitations that show up around a particular thing you desire, you are essentially, erasing and eliminating those blocks, Angles and limitations.

I invite you to bring up something in your life that isn't working for you. It could be anything, or you many have many things, but let's work with one for now. Make sure it is one that you feel very strongly about.

Ok, now as you began to think about those things, did you notice how your mood changed and your body felt? Perhaps your posture was different, or you felt a twinge of sadness, frustration, or angst? Could you feel yourself "sinking" or contracting? That "feeling" is the energy of that particular thing that you were thinking about; Each thing has its own energy.

Let's take shame... shame was always one of the biggies for me.

Shame is the lie someone told you about yourself. ANAIS NIN

Shame creates a limitation because it prevents us from receiving things that we hold in high regard. It speaks to feelings of unworthiness, alienation, isolation, loneliness, perfectionism, inferiority, helplessness, failure, self-doubt and/or deservingness.

As noted by Jonathan Bradshaw,

> "Guilt says I've done something wrong; shame says there is something wrong with me. Guilt says I've made a mistake; shame says I am a mistake. Guilt says what did was not good; shame says I am no good." Bradshaw (1988).

By "DE-LETING" that energy of shame, you are saying, everywhere I saw myself as flawed, wrong, undeserving, and limited myself because of that shame, I DELETE it. (I erase, cut and removed it) from my energetic flow.

DETECTOR OF TRUTH

What if I could give you an awesome foolproof tool that would allow you to know what is true for you in an instant, would you use it? Of course, I know many of you would say absolutely, "I'm game."

If you had such a tool, how would you be different? Ask yourself; "What would be different if I knew my unique truth?" Would you give yourself the freedom to choose those things that are in alignment with your truth; and not only change your world by example but change the world around you as well? Or would you just possess the tool, and change nothing, using it, to further entrain yourself of what is NOT possible for you?

It is vital that you know what is true for you, minus the thoughts and energies of others. If you never know what is true for you, how will you ever be able to align your outside world with your desires, and live the awesome life you were meant to live?

As noted author James Allen concluded,

"A man is not rightly conditioned until he is a happy, healthy, and prosperous being; and happiness, health, and prosperity are the result of a harmonious adjustment of the inner with the outer of the man with his surroundings."

Somehow, the general consensus is that if something is true, is should feel like a ton of bricks on your shoulders emotionally. Do you know someone, or are you that someone, who has felt "crushed" by the weight of information, a conversation or a communication? Maybe you thought something, like- "This must be true or else it wouldn't have hit me like a ton of bricks... or this is horrible, it must be true."

The odd part about this whole heaviness equals truth idea, is that, if the truth shall "set you free", how can you be free with a ton of bricks on your shoulders?

Just as heaviness has come to be associated with truth, the feeling of lightness has come to be associated with a lie, or not to be trusted.

I invite you to consider something. The word en*LIGHT*enment has come to represent an awakening to or illumination of, the truth. Note, that the word has *LIGHT* in it. The word is not *enHEAVYment*, right? So wouldn't it follow then, that what's true will make you feel **lighter**, and where something is heavy and dense it would be a lie?

He who knows others is wise. He who knows himself is enlightened.- Lao Tzu

One of the easiest ways to uncover what is your unique personal truth, is how you feel; Not in the context of a positive or negative emotion, but rather, a feeling of heavy or light.

The truth of a thing is the feel of it, not the think of it. *Stanley Kubrick*

Are you familiar with the phrases, a "heavy heart" or being "weighed down", and/or the "weight of the world on her shoulders"? These colloquialisms are great illustrations of how you feel when something IS NOT TRUE for you.

When you receive information from some person, place or thing, if it is not true, you will feel a sense of heaviness, confinement, and weighted. The energy is like a dense fog. If upon hearing something, you feel heavy, contracted and dense, it is a lie for you.

Comparatively, when something IS TRUE for you, you will feel light as a feather, dare I say, fluffy, and expansive. It is important to note, the feeling associated with your truth is neither good nor bad necessarily, it is just heavy or light.

Now there are times, based upon where you are in your "knowing of you" that you will feel light, and then seconds later become heavy. First, when you are using your Detector of Truth, gauge the IMMEDIATE feeling, before the doubts, fears and "how to's" creep in. In other words, don't take time to think about how you feel. Just feel how you feel and take note of your energy. What makes this tool so awesome is that it's not at all logical, so you cannot trick or manipulate it. You will feel heavier or lighter, based upon what is true for you. The tool does not require analysis and does not dwell in the "gray areas" of life.

Do you know someone, or are you someone, that has ever had an experience, where you were being told something, and you felt "that isn't true for me"; and you felt this way, despite evidence to the contrary? For example, you meet someone, and all of your family and friends tell you, "He's a great catch". Yet, somehow, you felt a heaviness or density about being with this person. There was nothing wrong with him, he was polite, and on paper a good catch, but you felt heavy. Rather, than following your truth, you decided to date him, and eventually for whatever reason, it didn't work out. You later made yourself wrong, because he was a "good" catch and then proceeded to judge yourself for not being able to make it work with such a "good catch".

Or perhaps, you have gone to a family event, and as soon as you arrived for that Christmas dinner, you felt a heaviness. Of course, you denied your truth, stayed there, all the while saying, something must be "wrong" with me, because I am not enjoying myself here"; another example, of going against your unique truth.

This tool can be applied to every aspect of your life. Perhaps you went to medical school but wanted to be a fashion designer. You completed it, but the entire process was arduous and laborious (compared to the normal stresses of medical school).Let's give the Detector of Truth a whirl, shall we?

ACTION STEP

Let's run through some thoughts and take particular note of how the thought or belief makes you feel. If you are a person that is visual, take a sheet a paper and write down the statements, then write next to the statement, HEAVY or LIGHT! Do not think, do not reason, do not ask, do not wonder, don't go what if, but if, should, could, maybe- Stick to HEAVY or LIGHT! No more, no less.

--They think I can't reach my goals.

--He thinks I am worthless.

--I keep failing at everything I try.

--She can do it, but, I know I can't.

--God is going to punish me.

--I should have known better.

--They think I should have known better.

--This wouldn't have happened, if I were a better person.

--I just keep making the same mistakes.

--I am depressed.

--I don't deserve a good life.

--I have made a lot of mistakes and now I have to live with them.

--It is too late for me.

--I made this bed and now I have to lie in it.

--Nothing ever changes.

--Nothing ever works out for me anyway.

--I try so hard but nothing happens.

--I am unlovable.

How did you feel? Did you feel heavy or light? Do you feel stretched and wide open or do you feel like your feet are in cement blocks. Would it even be safe to say, that you felt contracted? Like you wanted to crawl up somewhere, like a snail going into the shell?

The reason you felt so heavy, was because those statements were lies. The Divine truth of who you are, knows it's a lie, and was signaling to you, through the "weight" of the feeling, that it was not true for you. Whether you "believe" those things are who you are or not, the reality is, the most important part of you, the Divine part of you KNOWS that those things were not true.

ACTION STEP

Now, I want you to say these statements, and note whether they feel heavy or light. I suggest you write them down, just as you did with the statements above. These are not affirmations, so your focus on heavy or light, the feeling of contraction or expansion.

--I am unique.

--Anything is possible.

--I am lovable.

--I can do it!

--I rock!

--I am unstoppable!

--I would love to go for it!

--This time I am going BIG!

--There is nothing wrong with me

How did those statements feel? I know, just typing them brought a smile to my face. Did you feel lighter, more relaxed? Was there something inside you curious to know more?

It's worth noting- Any statement from your conscious mind, that comes up after your feeling of lightness or expansion that starts to disprove your lightness are lies. You've bought those lies as your truth and you are holding them in place with your judgments and conclusions about you. In the "C' section of RADICAL, and below, I will give you a shortcut to navigate and manage those nasty Energy Trolls and ANGLES.

As indicated in the "R" of RADICAL, it is important that you not blindly believe any and everything anyone says no matter the source. Your unique truth is essential to you being an expert on you. Using the Detector of Truth, is an excellent, practical, easy to use tool for assessing what may be your truth and what is a lie.

To recap- When someone says something that is true for you, you will feel like your body is opening and expanding, much like taking a deep cleansing breath and then releasing... a sort of "AHHHH".

If it feels heavy or dense, even if it is "good or bad", it is simply not true for you. It is important to note, that whether the answer is a yes or a no, doesn't make one better or worse than the other. This tool just allows you to feel what is true for you.

For instance, if I said, my grandfathers are dead, I feel lighter, because it is true. Make sense? If I were to say, that my grandfathers were alive, I would feel heavy because I know that they are both dead.

In other words, a yes is not better than no, or a right better than a wrong when using your Detector of Truth. Here is another illustration...

- If I were to say, I want to stay home and be a mom and pursue no outside interests of my own other than my children. I would feel as heavy as Andre the Giant. While there are women and men that, the above statement may be true for, it is NOT true for me. A no is just as true as a yes. Do you see how this works? Simple, right?

In other words, when you hear information, imagine it is a coat and put the coat on your body. How does that coat feel? Do you feel light or heavy? Do you feel bolder, braver, are you standing more erect? Are you feeling powerful and an immediate sense of relief and "lightness"? If so, the information is more likely true for you

If you feel heavy and weighted down by it, chances are, it is not true for you. Now, when using this technique you must be mindful, that sometimes, based on our conditioning, something may feel heavy then light or light then heavy or a combination of the two. When this is the case, you have to go to what you desire, as was the case for me, a baby, and ask, "Which information is more in line with what I desire?", and then take action based upon that.

Another way to get maximum benefit from your Detector of Truth, is to frame the situation or circumstance in the form of a question. For example, say, "Truth, do I want to__(fill in the blank).

However, sense many of us, are asking contracting, non-expansive questions, we are stuck in a non-expansive place. I will discuss asking questions of your Detector of Truth for maximum benefit in the "C" section of this book.

William James says it so wonderfully,

"Seek out that particular mental attribute which makes you feel most deeply and vitally alive, along with which comes the inner voice which says, 'This is the real me,' and when you have found that attitude, follow it."

STEP 4. "I"= "I" IS ALWAYS FIRST + INTUITION

"I" is ALWAYS FIRST

"The most influential person you will talk to all day is you." Zig Ziglar

"No one can give you better advice than yourself." Cicero

Wise words from Zig Ziglar, right? Not too bad from Cicero either. Sadly, it took the devastating losses of those 5 precious babies that forced me to take a moment of pause and say, WHAT THE HELL?

For as much as I thought myself a "free thinker", the glaring reality was I was buying ANGLES and points of view from any one selling them. Sure, I wasn't necessarily a Kool-Aid drinker but I wasn't listening to my own voice, or thinking for myself.

"To find yourself, think for yourself." Socrates

Now, that you know how points of view and ANGLES create your reality, I share in all candor, that I was just one of the bison going over the cliff with the rest of the heard, and calling it my life

Let me explain.

Native Americans in their infinite genius realized that Bison (American Buffalo), were a necessary and indispensible part of their survival. Obviously, given the size and speed of Bison, Native Americans had to come up with creative ways to get the "hunting" advantage. They devised, a sort of hunting ruse, where members of the tribe would create a stampede by dressing up as wolves and Bison.

Apparently Bison, don't l o o k up when they are a part of the pack, they just keep moving. As decoys, the Native Americans, would herd the Bison towards a cliff, where the Bison would just jump off cliff, either to their immediate death, or broken legs. Other tribe members would be waiting at the bottom of the cliff for the dead or immobilized Bison, and the

Native Americans then would be able to use the Bison from the rooter to the tooter- using the bones for weapons, hooves for glue, and the meat for food.[14]

Suffice it to say, I was a bison, and unfortunately, many of us are Bison. Certainly, neither you nor I will be jumping off any cliffs, (hopefully), but it is easier than you think to stop thinking for yourself, since often times you aren't even aware that you are doing it. We just go through the day like energetic satellites, picking up the thoughts and feelings of those around us and the AOI thinking they are ours. It gets you thinking right?

Value your own opinion more, and others' opinions less. - Jonathan Lockwood Huie

Consider this, when confronted with having to make a decision, what do you do first? Do you immediately get on your cell, and call your friends and ask them what they think about it? Or do you get an idea and sort of sit with it for a while?

In today's world, do you post something in your personal status on Facebook, so your "friends" can offer their blind guidance and commentary? Do you send out a tweet? How many times a day, week, month, do you find yourself saying to someone else, "What do you think about________? What would you do if__________?" What is the first thing you do, honestly?

When faced with a challenge or "difficult situation", the natural and cultural inclination is to IMMEDIATELY seek the advice of someone else. Let's look at that for a second. We are conditioned to call upon someone outside of ourselves to answer a question that relates to ourselves.

It is one thing to share some good news with a family or friend, but life changing decisions, well, we don't consult our "inner expert", we look for answers from someone else. Why is that? After all, each one of us is unique, and living one's own life is entirely subjective; yet many rely on the opinions of others for important life decisions.

I am not suggesting that if you are an "I first" thinker, that you should not gather objective data, get learned advice from similarly situated people, who have successfully managed the life conundrum you now find yourself in. What I am saying, is to gather information objectively, and run it past your Detector of Truth, and then make a decision. No one knows better than you, what is true for you.

An "I first" thinker, simply means, that you honor your truth above anyone else's. No one knows what you know, NO ONE! You are the expert on you and everything else, is simply data.

"To go against the dominant thinking of your friends, of most of the people you see every day, is perhaps the most difficult act of heroism you can perform"- Theodore H. White

I have always felt like I was on the "outside" of life. Saddled with tons of "family secrets", didn't help my "outsider" life, that's for sure. I grew up with so much shame and self-disdain blaming myself for the things that were happening to me. I just wanted someone to like me; someone to think that I was good and special; for someone to validate my existence. This obsession with being liked cost me dearly; No doubt it cost me happiness, passion and potential... losing those babies was certainly the ultimate price.

I BLINDLY, yes BLINDLY followed the advice of my doctors, because I wanted them to think that I was a "good patient" and easy to deal with. Like the Bison, I put my head down and went over the cliff.

During my "baby quest", my first 3 losses, were because I took medication, that I knew in every fiber of my being, I should not take. The doctor told me it would be "fine", but that quiet loving voice inside me, said, "Tiph, don't do it, just wait a few weeks"... I didn't listen to me. I wasn't an "I first thinker"... My truth was saying, "Tiph, don't go over the cliff!"

Again, this is not to say, that they were bad people, or intended harm. The thing is, when I received their information, before I put that pill in my mouth, I still had the choice of "I first"- my knowing, my truth, my beliefs.

I went against myself and took the medication. With the loss of the Twin Angels, exams were performed because it was "customary", and I allowed it to happen. From those experiences, I had to learn that no one is more of an expert on me, than me! I know what my body is capable of, because I control the switchboard, MY MIND! I had a right to be an *"I first thinker"*... it's not a privilege but a RIGHT!

Since being from and for yourself is a right, it begs the question, why are most of us Bison? Why aren't we *"I first thinkers"?*

I know one of the reasons, is that we don't want to appear selfish. Another reason, is we sadly don't trust ourselves to know what is right for us. If you are a "consulter", ask yourself, why you would think that someone outside of you, would know more about you <u>than</u> you? How is that possible? You are with you, 24/7 days per week, 365 days in a non-leap year.

Again, I want to be absolutely clear, I am by no means suggesting, stating, or concluding, that you shouldn't gather objective data. What I am inviting you to do, is to take a moment, feel what's true and receive those thoughts, because those are YOUR thoughts. Do you feel heavy or light? Follow the energy that makes you feel expansive, light and open- follow your truth.

Consider this- if you check in with your truth, and follow that energy, you will know who you need to consult that will add value to you, further expanding the possibilities to bring your desires to you. Your truth will open the Universe's toolbox to create the synchronicities that will further enable you to achieve, do, and be the thing you are seeking. For example, by listening to ME, I was able to discover an all-natural herbal remedy that enabled me to get pregnant, stay pregnant and deliver wonderfully healthy babies. When I was asked by someone, how in the world I found that herbal remedy, I told her, “I have no idea”.

Your truth will enable to you connect with those that have been successful in that particular area, rather than those that are struggling with no end in sight.

I invite you to do the following:

For the next week, before you go to consult with someone about something in your life, stop and ask yourself, “What do I know to be true about this? Notice your immediate energy. The great Jim Rohn has said, that there are 3 questions to ask yourself that will assist you in resolving any challenge, *“…First, what could I do? Second, what could I read? And third, who could I ask?”*

It is no accident, that the first two questions, involved the “I” first. Knowledge can certainly come from others, but truth, joy always comes from within.

Thinking for yourself is your Divine Right, it is one of the greatest gifts that we have as humans. In the age with information, literally at your fingertips, it is so easy to just be told, what you “should” do or “how” to live to be happy. Add to that the habitual patterns of our AOI, and what you are left with, is a sort of self-awareness laziness. Many people are simply looking for others to tell them how to live. It could be because of fear of being wrong, not wanting to hurt someone’s feelings, wanting to belong, and of course, not trusting one’s self.

Consider this- being an “I first thinker” is the only way to live a fulfilling life. While you may “feel” selfish, you are actually protecting yourself and others by taking responsibility for your thinking and actions taken based upon your thinking. Live and love freely, as you will be less likely to resent your family’s bad advice, or the feeling that you are being manipulated through their advice for their own personal benefit. “I first” thinking, sets clear boundaries for you and for them. Simply stated, “I first” thinking gives you freedom.

It would be safe to say based on my experience in coaching, consulting and just plain living, that there are some of you who believe that you do make your own decisions and there is "no harm" in getting feedback from the people you love. There may also be some of you, that are offended that I would even suggest that you aren't an "I first" thinker. Below are some questions to consider if you are an *"I first thinker"*.

ACTION STEP: "I First" Tester Questions

Again, I want you to consider the following:

--Whenever you ask for advice, ask yourself, "Why" are you even asking? For confirmation or out of no self-trust? Do you have specific people that you ask specific things?

--Do you ask for advice on social media regarding something pressing and important, even in jest?

--Do you immediately call a family member for advice in love, career, or other life conundrums?

--How often do say the words: "What do you think about this situation/circumstance/person/incident /conversation? What would you do if this or that happened to you?

--Do you limit your options based on conventional wisdom?

--Do you think about how others' will feel, think or do if you would think for yourself?

--How often do you make decisions based upon your past?

--Do you do things because "they have always been done that way?"--When you seek "feedback", do you give the person all of the information necessary? Or do you give them just enough information to try and create the answer you want?

--Do you let others, sway you away from doing what you know is true and right for you?

--How often do you consult superstition, old wives' tales, and the ramblings of your "great aunt"?

--Do you justify in your mind, why someone else's opinions are right for you?

--Does the old adage, "Who are you trying to convince, me or yourself..." ever apply to you? Meaning, you try to convince someone else, to also convince yourself

--If someone asks you why you are thinking a certain way, do you wince or shrink? Does it affect your confidence?

--When someone offers "feedback", do you immediately feel their ideas are "better" than yours?

--Do you ask for permission? Do you often say, "Would that be alright with you?"

--Do you respond to someone saying something like: "I'm sorry, I just think my way is good enough?" (By apologizing, you are diminishing yourself and not being an "I first thinker")

--How many people do you check in with and get "feedback" from before you make a decision? I am not referring to gathering "data" or experimental information gathering.

--Do you go from person to person relaying what the other person who offered "feedback" said? AKA Gossiping

You do not need anyone's permission to be your true self. Jonathan Lockwood Huie

INTUITION

"The intellect has little to do on the road to discovery. There comes a leap in consciousness, call it intuition or what you will, and the solution comes to you, and you don't know how or why." Albert Einstein
"Intuition will tell the thinking mind where to look next." Jonas Salk

If you ask ten people their definition of intuition, I guarantee it's likely you'll receive 10 different definitions. The consensus however, is that intuition is a sort of instinctive knowing. Amazingly, despite any logical reasoning, our intuition is able to acquire then produce knowledge in any given moment.

Given that our intuition isn't necessarily polluted by ANGLES and energy trolls, it is in most ways, the purest thoughts and *awareness'* we have; in my estimation the most reliable wisdom there is.

Our intuition is the mental faculty with which we are able to perceive and tune into the energy of someone or someplace. Intuition, is the direct perception of truth or fact independent of any reasoning or involvement of the rational or logical mind. The word itself, is derived from the Latin root, "*intueri*", which roughly translates "to look inside".[15]

As an inner guide, your intuition guides you to your best self via your choices, actions and choosing what feels light or heavy, i.e. truth or lies.

Anytime, we can remove analysis or our logical conscious minds, and allow our inner knowing to make a decision, we grow spiritually and create a trust with ourselves, that will make us UNSTOPPABLE!

Often times, I am asked, "How do I know when my intuition

speaks?" One of the sweetest people I know, even asked, "Do I have intuition?" Each and every one of us has intuition. Since each of us is unique how and the means by which we receive it is different.

Many of us, were raised to not listen to our "inner voice" or own truth. Consequently, we are waiting for a loud bullhorn of judgment, that says, "NO, STOP, or GO RIGHT, YOU ARE MAKING A MISTAKE"! I can assure you- that is NOT your intuition speaking to you, especially, if it's yelling and filled with judgment.

Our intuition is a subtle, yet powerful voice. It does not sound like our parents, pastors, teachers, or friends.

Intuition by its inside nature, will be experienced by you in your inner voice- in YOUR OWN voice. Our intuition is positive and encouraging, not fearful and timid. Intuition would not motivate you via fear; more on fear and intuition in a moment.

Although our intuition will speak to each of us differently, there is one fundamental truth about our intuition- it will speak in a quiet, encouraging tone, to expand you, stretch you to explore new things to grow and will resonate deep within you; you will know, without knowing how or why. It will "feel right", even in those times when it doesn't feel "good.

Fear is often confused or becomes entangled with intuition. Let me be absolutely clear, where life or limb is at stake, reasonable fear may very well be your intuition speaking to you. In those cases, it is not really "fear", but awareness.

Check this out- have you heard, or have you ever experienced a serious major challenge? Did you freak out or did you get calm and handle it? I'm sure you've at least read stories about people doing seemingly impossible things when faced with a crisis, right? It was as if time slowed down and another level of consciousness kicked it, right? Ok, so if fear were "real" wouldn't a time of crisis be a time to have fear? How it is that one can be totally calm in a situation that would be "fearful"? What if fear was actually a lie? Is it possible that what you fear, may just be greater awareness, a higher level of consciousness?

In this book, I am specifically referring to the fear, that keeps you stuck, makes you feel contracted and self- protective and languishing inside your "comfort zone." For you see, the life of your dreams is invariably outside your comfort zone.

"You have to leave the city of your comfort and go into the wilderness of your intuition. What you'll discover will be wonderful. What you'll discover is yourself." Alan Alda

Thankfully, our intuition can be cultivated and strengthened, just as our physical muscles in the body. The more you listen to your intuition, the more in tune with your inner knowing and guide you become. As you begin to follow your inner knowing, you will grow in your trust of YOU! YAY!

I must admit that my intuition muscles were as weak as Alfalfa in the Little Rascals! I did not trust my inner voice at all! When you don't value or believe yourself worthy, certainly, anything that originates with you- is not to be trusted. I ALWAYS sought the approval of others, and/or allowed their opinions to ultimately be my decisions. Even when I knew, in every ounce of my being it would come back and bite me.

Back when I lost my Twin Angels, my intuition was lovingly speaking to me every moment of every hour, and I would literally shut it down. When I was pregnant with the Twin Angels, my well-meaning Dr., prescribed some invasive procedures for me, based upon "his determination" that I was "high risk". Here again, I relied on his assessment and opinions, rather than my own inner-knowing. I witnessed some questionable hygiene practices by the ER physicians, and technicians and said nothing! For example, one doctor put on a sterile glove and then grabbed his chair where God only knows how many bacteria were and then used the same glove for a vaginal exam. I was thinking at the time, "he has been sitting there and God knows who else, he should change his glove, before doing this vaginal exam." Yet, I said NOTHING! I was paralyzed, my body was telling me to speak up, say something, and walk out. Seriously, how hard would it have been to ask the DR to put on a new glove? Even though I wanted to scream, WHAT THE FUCK??? I stuffed down my intuition, my inner knowing and what I knew to be true for me. Ultimately, me not listening, resulted in an infection, to one of the Twin Angeles, and consequently, both Angeles had to be delivered prematurely- despite one of the babies being PERFECTLY healthy.

It is absolutely worth noting, that the pathology report, revealed that those Twin Angeles were PERFECT in every way. They were beautiful, just born too soon. I must tell you, there is no pain, like the pain of delivering babies that you know will take one breathe and pass right before your eyes.

Now by comparison, with Bliss, Strycker and Spring, I was a RADICAL SELF-EXPERT; simply stated, I was a ROCK STAR in my life's production… a legend in my own shower!

If it wasn't in line with what my inner knowing said, I would not do it. If I saw a practice by one of the physicians, that I deemed hygienically unacceptable, I demanded they put on another set of gloves; if the sheet didn't look clean enough, I wouldn't sit on it. There were NO vaginal exams unless absolutely necessary and an external ultrasound was inconclusive.

Now, many of you, may see this as extreme, but again, I knew what was right for me, and anything less was UNACCEPTABLE. You have to trust your inner knowing, your intuition. You are the authority and expert on YOU! The trick is to not cloud your intuition in negative thoughts or emotions. Your intuition is NOT fear or doubt based. It is strong and powerful.

I love the quote by Anne Wilson, *"Trusting our intuition often saves us from disaster."* In my case, truer words have never been spoken.

ACTION STEP

Answer the Following Questions-

Do you know what your intuition is?

Do you regularly connect with your intuition? Do you listen to your intuition?

Where you have you disregarded or stuffed down your intuition?

What does your intuition "sound" like? Whose voice is it?

How does it communicate with you?

Flex Your Intuition...Some Intuition Building Exercises

"You must train your intuition - you must trust the small voice inside you which tells you exactly what to say, what to decide" *Ingrid Bergman*

1. Acknowledge that your intuition is there and a key player in your life.
2. Take notice of all the ways your intuition attempts t o communicate and connect with you throughout the day.
3. Look for evidence of when you're listening to intuition.
4. Don't overcomplicate things. The key to intuition is simplicity
5. Learn to trust your gut feelings.
6. Release thinking that your intuition will show up in a particular way or a particular voice.

7. Listen to your intuition.
8. Release the desire to be "right".

"Intuition is a spiritual faculty and does not explain, but simply points the way." Florence Scovel Shinn

In-tuition vs. Out-tuition

Some people refer to things like the Ego, super-ego and the like. I found it much more helpful to speak more plainly. For me, there is *IN-tuition* and Out-tuition. *In-tuition* is my inner knowing and always originates from within and Out-tuition is everything else.

For those of us with some self-trust issues, intuition is difficult to come by. Prior to becoming a Radical Self-Expert, I made a point to "push down" my intuition because I honestly believed that other people knew more about me than I did. I relied on *Out-tuition.*

In my own quest to truly understand, access, and develop my intuition, I was led to what I call *"Intuition Pointers"*. These are like training wheels for intuition development. They "point" you more or less in the direction of intuition or OUT-tuition (coming from someplace other than deep inside of YOU).

A few are original, and a few are things that I picked up along my journey to being a Radical Self-Expert. They felt light for me, and so they are true for me. I invite you to use mine and of course develop your own. It is important to remember, that I cannot tell you definitely what your IN-tuition pointers are, as each person receives and communicates with their IN-tuition, in their unique way. However, I invite you to use and expand on the pointers.

IN-tuition Pointers:

--In-tuition is genuine, coming from a place of security and safety. It does not see me as a wounded survivor of childhood abuse in need of protection. My guidance sees me as whole, complete and perfect.

--In-tuition is not about me gaining control over anyone or anything, but rather just wants me to express my divinity and Infinite True Self.

--IN-tuition is not flaky or wishy-washy.

--IN-tuition is GUIDANCE not direction. It doesn't tell me what to do step by step. Rather, it reminds me of my Divinity as a child of the Divine.

--It does not tell me to go after happiness that is outside of me, but rather joy from within me.

--I feel joyful and uplifted when I receive Guidance from my intuition. It is NOT heavy or doubting.

--My intuition is more grounded in my stomach, or deep inside my solar plexus. Often it originates in my stomach and move to my tailbone.

--When my In-tuition "speaks" to me, it is usually my voice I hear. It is not the voice of God, or someone from my past, or even from my present. It is my own voice.

OUT-tuition Pointers

-- OUT-tuition usually comes in the form of a directive and filled with judgment. It refers me back to my past "mis-takes".

--My Out-tuition is physically felt in my head or shoulders, some place higher than in my "gut"

-OUT-tuition focuses on the "how", rather than my "what".

--OUT-tuition assumes that the world is an unsafe place, that I'm weak and need to be protected.

--OUT-tuition directs me more towards external validation or external results in order to "feel good".

--OUT-tuition focuses more on competitiveness and labels.

--OUT-tuition is the lawyer side of me. It is always making a case for something.

--Out-tuition focuses on the "rightness and wrongness" of the situation. In other words, it is full of stories, judgments and conclusions all of which cut off the infinite supply of possibilities.

--When OUT-tuition speaks, it is usually someone else's voice, a person (s) who has a lot of judgments about me- sisters, parents, etc.

-- If at any point, you go to "...because", this is out-tuition.

Again, use your Detector of Truth to access your IN-tuition and OUT-tuition.

"Just be honest with yourself. That opens the door." Vernon Howard

STEP 5. C= CURIOSITY + CURIOUS LIVING

"Curiosity is one of the permanent and certain characteristics of a vigorous mind." Samuel Johnson

Creative thinking begins with great questions, not answers. Great creative thinkers stay with the question instead of rushing to find an immediate solution. They ask more questions than the average person and are comfortable in the often uncomfortable situation of not immediately having the answer." Elaine Dundon

Curiosity has gotten a bad rap. How many times, have we either heard or read the saying" Curiosity killed the cat?" Interestingly, it is undisputed that genius is born out of curiosity.

When I refer to being curious, I am speaking not of butting into other people's business or being a pain in the butt busy-body. As I said, the "I" is always first, so getting into someone else's affairs, is not my concern here.

By curious, I mean consistently and continuously asking and living via empowering questions without necessarily going directly to the answer. Asking and living a question from a space of general sense of wonderment- a sort of surprise you are waiting to receive from the Universe.

Let's dive deeper into the "mechanics" of what I call CURIOUS LIVING

CURIOSITY RE-DEFINED

Albert Einstein stated, *"I have no special talent. I am only passionately curious".* Curiosity opens the mind, creates space and attracts new ideas.

Curious living, enables you to know what only you know, and to know that you know by asking empowering questions. Your power to change everything in your life, rests in you being the gift that you truly "BE"; Success, fulfillment, happiness, joy, freedom, and power, only flow from who you truly are. It doesn't flow from who you have perceived yourself to be from another person's perspective, conditioning, or their judgments, assumptions and limitations.

Energy is never at rest, and is constantly vibrating, right? Curious living invites the free flow of energy and allows you to move from opinions, conclusions, assumptions, judgments and points of views, to possibilities. It creates the space for you to be totally aware in any given moment, rather than somewhere locked in the past of what was and could have been.

When you live curiously, something magical happens. You bring everything to your life with ease and grace, because you are no longer pushing, pulling, and battling with "trying to make something work".

"Ask, and it shall be given you; seek; and you shall find; knock and it shall be opened unto you. For every one that asketh receiveth; and he that seeketh findeth; and to him that knocketh it shall be opened." Matthew 7:7-8 –Bible

Although the principle of "Ask and You Shall Receive" is generally associated with that passage in the Bible, it is invariably a universal law. We ask a question to receive something, correct? Where in that passage or universal law does it say, "Conclude to receive, opine, or judge and receive"? It doesn't. This is why it is important to live curiously. What is true, is that the Universe is infinite and you are a part of that universe. Whether you refer to the Universe as God, Your Higher Self, Jehovah, Mother Earth, the Divine, or however you identify that which is beyond your limited understanding, you are directly connected to "IT".

When you ask a question with genuine wonderment because the Universe is limitless, there are infinite ways upon which that thing that you are seeking can actualize for you. Questions by their very nature expand what is possible. There are no less than a million ways, something could show up, but when you try and answer your own question, the answer you are seeking is limited only to what you can see as possible.

"The power to question is the basis of all human progress." Indira Gandhi

When you begin living curiously, without going directly to what you think should be or is the answer, the Universe is eager to respond to your questions energetically, in the form of opportunities, people, or places that will not only give you an "answer", but something even greater.

"We keep moving forward, opening new doors, and doing new things, because we're curious and curiosity keeps leading us downnewpaths."WaltDisney

The power is in the asking of the empowering question, rather than immediately searching for an answer. Many of you are probably thinking, "Well, I ask questions all the time, but I don't feel free or light, I just feel hopeless!" My question to you would be, "what types of questions are you asking?"

Are you making statements and then throwing a question mark at the end? Let's be clear, I am not referring to the "Why am I such a loser, or why can't I keep a man, or why can't I (fill in the blank)" type questions. Do you feel powerful when you ask those questions? Of course you don't!

"It is not the answer that enlightens, but the question. " Eugene Ionesco

The Anatomy of A Question:

I think a dissection of the Stages of a Question is in Order Here:

*****BONUS Benefit—Asking empowering questions, By-Passes the Energy Trolls of Judgment and Fear. YAY!***

For you see, when you ask a question, your subconscious mind, (yes the same one from your awareness that if left uncheck can wreak havoc) immediately begins looking for an answer. You don't even have to consciously believe the question you are asking because the mind isn't designed for believing questions, only for searching for answers.

Below, is a simple dissection of how many people typically ask questions... The sample question is: "Why can't I ever get what I want in my life?"

Typical Question Dissection- STAGES of a QUESTION:

Question: Why can't I ever get what I want in my life?

Stage 1: The word "Why" sends a message to your brain to start looking for answers. Why is like the search function on the computer. A question with the word why, immediately starts to look for answers. It needs to answer why.

Stage 2: "Can't I ever"- Now in this stage of the question, "can't I ever" is telling your brain to go to the archives or hard drive. You are directing your attention to the memory bank. So you just typed into your mental computer search box -"go the memory bank". The memory bank is NOT forward thinking in possibilities. It can only use what it knows to go and get, based solely on your command.

Stage 3: "Get What I Want"- In this third stage, your question is complete. You are pushing enter on your mental computer. The results are in, and because you looked to your memory bank... i.e., looked backward for an answer, you will get things like, because you don't deserve it. Or you dig deep into your memory archives for every time you didn't get something and your memory will be something like, ... "because she was better than you", or "you haven't pay enough dues yet", or "when you changed before your friends got mad..." and so and so

Stage 4: Finally, with every retrieved answer, the brain gains momentum and now starts kicking out, everything you ever done

EVER in your life, to answer your single question, "Why can't I ever get what I want in my life" There is a laundry list of why you can't ever get what you want. Notice, none of those things look into the future. They are all based on the past.

Now, when you brain begins to go to the archives of your life, do you feel heavy or light? Heavy, right?

Quick Recap on the Role of the Subconscious Mind-

The subconscious mind is like the hard drive on your laptop with enormous disk space. On it, are your experiences, learned habits, programming, and all of the perceptions, conclusions, ANGLES, points of view and observations from your five senses. There is an enormous archive of your life on this hard drive. It has no analytical ability, and simply stores information, which will be played back on demand by the conscious mind.

Given, it is ONLY a playback device- past stuff in, past stuff out... disempowering stuff in, disempowering stuff out. It does not filter or analyze any information. Think LAPTOP!

Here is a personal example of the power of questions...

One of my old playback questions was: "Why do bad things ALWAYS happen to me?"

Question- Why are these bad things ALWAYS happening to me?

1. Asking "WHY" immediately sent my brain into overdrive to find the answer.
2. "ALWAYS"- now my brain in scouring the hard drive for reasons, conclusions, computations and judgments to answer the ALWAYS. It is digging deep in the old memory drive to justify the always to my WHY.
3. "Bad things Happen to Me"- Question complete, and answer is expected immediately

    [Side note- Remember, I have been trained from an early age, to "get an answer quickly" and the reward will be, not having to wonder why. This is a huge reward, because being in a space of unknown used to be unbearable.]

4. Now that my question is my complete, my brain goes to the answer based on all of the conclusions, judgments, and "stuff" on the hard-drive. ANSWER: Tiphanie, bad things ALWAYS happen to you, because of karma, remember when you lied, this is your pay back.... You are bad, if you were good, then the bad things wouldn't happen to you. You are not good enough, you don't deserve it, remember that time when...? You are just not good at making good decisions, everything always blows up in your face... Everyone is better than you, no one likes you, and you suck"

YIKES! Yes, those were actual answers to one of my disempowering questions. It goes without saying, that at no point did I feel light or expansive with those questions or answers.

Those types of "harmless" questions, keep you stuck in your past, "mis-takes". They are replete with judgment and conclusions. The above question is an illustration of a question that is backward looking which trigger its own set of answers; which then leads to certain feelings that then lead to certain actions or inactions, which can only produce certain types of results.

What is so awesome, is that the subconscious mind, doesn't know, good or bad, it just plays information. So, if you start out each and every day, by asking empowering expansive questions, your subconscious mind, will immediately begin to work just the same.

Simply stated, ask a "good" question, and you will receive a "good answer". I am sure you have heard the phrase, "what you sew you reap", right?

Even more awesome, is that the empowering question, may in fact, BE the energetic answer you were seeking. How cool is that? More on your receiving "answers" to follow.

If you are thinking, "ok Tiphanie, if not those questions, then which ones?" That in and of itself is an empowering question, because you are seeking tools which will give you greater insight into you and all of the possibilities that are available to you. YAY!

Empowering expansive questions create the space for you to receive the gifts from the Universe. Think of things this way- if you are already holding in both hands the answer to the question, how can the Universe give you another one. Analogously, if you ask an expansive empowering question, it empties your hands to receive from the Universe in the infinite ways that only the Universe can deliver to you. ASK and YOU SHALL RECEIVE!

****NOTE:** You don't have to consciously believe your empowering questions for them to be effective. Our minds are not designed to believe the questions, but rather, to seek answers to the questions posed it.

A question from a space of curiosity, expansion and possibility contains these 6 elements:

1. Simple
2. Specific
3. Light and expansive
4. Curious
5. Generates possibilities and energy
6. Looks Forward

Remember from your Detector of Truth, the truth will always make you feel light and spacious and a lie will make you feel closed, trapped heavy and contracted.

Notice I didn't say positive or negative? Only look for what makes you feel light(er) or heavy(ier). Light and heavy as a gauge for what is your truth is an excellent tool to use for asking and receiving energetic answers to your questions. The most awesome benefit of this tool, is it reminds you of just how powerful you are and that every "answer" you were always searching for, was inside of you all along!

While your DETECTOR of TRUTH, is extremely effective by itself, let's add some juice to it, with a little TRUTH Calibration. To get a barometer of what feels heavy and light as it relates to Curious Living, let's try on some Curious Living questions just for kicks.

Ask yourself the questions below and notice how you feel. Notice if you feel expansive, spacious and light, or heavy and dense.

ACTION STEP: PART I

With that in mind, notice how these questions make you feel:

- Why can't I seem to do anything right?

-Why am I still single? or Why do I stay with him/ her when everything is telling me to leave?

-Why can't I make a relationship work?

-Why do I always end up getting cheated on?

-Why am I so unlucky?

How do those questions feel? Heck, just typing those questions, had me weighted down. Did you feel contracted and closed? Perhaps your shoulders slumped a bit? Now, you know what a "lie" or heaviness feels like.

By comparison, ask yourself the questions below, and note how you feel?

ACTION STEP: PART I I.

Ask Yourself The Questions Below:

-What juicy adventures and experiences will I get into today?

-What else is possible for me and my life?

-What awesomeness awaits me?

-How could I raise my energy right now?

-What kind of energy can I create that will bring me everything I desire?

-How can my life get any better?

-Who would I be without my judgments?

-How can I make this moment orgasmic for me?

-What would it take to receive love from someone who is willing to receive all of me?

After reading those questions, did you feel lighter?

Really pay attention to your energy. Your true energy will guide you towards the things that most resonate with you as the uniquely Divine Being that you are.

Here are Some Sample Curious Living Questions to Get You Started Every Morning & Before You Fall Asleep

- How does it get even better than this?
- How could it possibly get better than this?
- What else is possible here?

- How could this turn out even better than anything I could ever imagine and more…
- What awesomeness would I like to show up in my life today?
- What could I ask the universe that would and could expand my life beyond my wildest dreams?
- What would it take for more yummy things to show up?
- What is it that I know, that if I acknowledged that I know, would change everything in my life?
- If I knew how much of a gift and contribution I was to the world, how much would I allow myself to receive?

"Questions are the creative acts of intelligence." Joan Borysenko

Never stop asking questions. Heck, even when the "answer" shows up, ask another question like, "how does it get even better or more delicious? Or how could there be any more YAY today?" You asked, so the Universe will respond and show you! Isn't that wonderful??? How cool is that?

"The purpose of questioning is to help you think uncommonly about common problems. Also, asking the right questions helps you to find, formulate and focus your ideas." Grace McCartland

Simply stated, *Curious Living*, means that you are living as if you know nothing, and receive everything from Your True Self. How would curious living transform your life and your vision of who you are and how you exist in the world?

Surely, this is an important step in becoming an Expert in You. When you ask expansive empowering questions, you are literally living in the land of possibilities.

"Become a possibilitarian. No matter how dark things seem to be or actually are, raise your sights and see possibilities - always see them, for they're always there."*Norman Vincent Peale*

Opinions, conclusions, and rushing to "figure it out", cut off the receiving of all the possibilities. As noted by Jim Rohn, *"Asking is the beginning of receiving. Make sure you don't go to the ocean with a teaspoon. At least take a bucket so the kids won't laugh at you."*

The idea of living curiously may be a bit confusing as we are often praised for having the answer, and having it quickly. I know personally, in my third grade class with Mrs. Alexander, I would win the math challenges, because I had the answer quicker than my fellow students. It is not surprising, that the number of questions we ask in a day decreases with age just as cynicism, judgments and opinions, increase each day with age.

Children have an innate curiosity and correspondingly, live in the world of limitless possibilities. When we are children, we believe anything is possible until someone tells us otherwise; trees can talk, friends are invisible, yet still very much alive and real, and one can be an actor, judge, singer and fireman all at the same time, "when I grow up".

I remember believing that when I grew up I would become a doctor or scientist; that was until I had a teacher who told me that Blacks were not good at science, so I would have to work extra hard to compete with the white kids. OUCH! Can you imagine? Today, I am sure that teacher would be fired or minimally reprimanded.

This point also ties into the power of ANGLES, and buying them as our own. That teachers ANGLE of what was possible for me, became my awareness, and my scientist dreams died. My curiosity for math and science ended with her lack of belief right then. As a side note, I am not sure why she had that ANGLE about Blacks, and in particular me, because I was a top student, and skipped the 4th grade entirely, because of my grades and IQ. Just goes to show, that conclusions answers and judgments, tend to be limiting, irrational and baseless in most instances.

How would your life be different if you engaged in curious living? The benefits of CURIOUS LIVING are immeasurable. If you are asking expansion empowering questions as you move through life, everything in your life becomes expansive. Your mind is open to all that life is and what you make it to be. You will feel a sense of lightness and peace, as your energy will be high, and there is no space for judgment of yourself or others.

The How To's of CURIOUS LIVING

Firstly, when you encounter information, don't blindly accept it as fact because of the bearer of that information. Inquire within in the form of an expansive question, whether that information is true FOR YOU.

Secondly, live each and every day from that of a curious investigator exploring infinite possibilities, eagerly awaiting the arrival of coming attractions AND more.

The important thing is not to stop questioning. Curiosity has its own reason for existing. One cannot help but be in awe when he contemplates the mysteries of eternity, of life, of the marvelous structure of reality. It is enough if one tries merely to comprehend a little of this mystery every day. Never lose a holy curiosity. Albert Einstein

Thirdly, choose questions that are empowering, uplifting and expansive. Use your Detector of Truth, to determine what is true for you. Go to questions that make you feel light, rather than dense and heavy.

Lastly, do not answer the question. Allow yourself to remain in the unknown and receive. I like to think of the "unknown" as the *Possibility Zone*. Feel into what is true for you. An infinite question is so often destroyed by a finite answer, conclusion or judgment. Curiously live!

Clever people seem not to feel the natural pleasure of bewilderment, and are always answering questions when the chief relish of a life is to go on asking them. Frank Moore Colby

Curious living, is not making a statement then throwing a question mark at the end. That is to say, that if you are asking a question with a pre-determined outcome that is not *living curiously*, but instead a statement, judgment, or conclusion with a question mark at the end. The energy should be one of a genuine expansion of possibilities and space.

The power is always in the asking, when in doubt, remember, one of the laws of the Universe, is to ASK and RECEIVE, not answer and receive. Empowering questions allow you to expand, while answers bring you back to finite thinking.

"Nothing shapes our lives so much as the questions we ask." Sam Keen

Living curiously is important in becoming a Radical Self-Expert, as the questions create space to receive. It empties your energetic hands, so you can receive your energetic answers based upon your unique truth. Once you receive energetically, you can think take actions in alignment with your truth. How rad is that?

Try to love the questions themselves...Do not now look for the answers... It is a question of experiencing everything... At present you need to live the question...Ranier Maria Rilke

If you ask a question, and notice you feel contracted, heavy or almost trapped, you know whatever you perceive isn't TRUE for you. Accordingly, you can take action based solely on YOUR truth, which will invariably lead you to greater peace, happiness, success, fulfillment, and beyond. Financial, spiritual, emotional, physical and psychological success can flow only from who YOU are truly

Curious living, enables you to focus only on what is important to you, free from the beliefs and thoughts of others, society, media, your past, and all other external influences.

Questions wake us up. They open our eyes and our ears, our minds and our hearts. They plow the fertile fields of our thinking, preparing the field for the idea seeds that will be dropped from a chance encounter, a passing bird or a gentle breeze." Joyce Wycoff

Many of you are probably saying, "Ok Tiph, I get it, but how will I know the "answer" to what I need to do next?"

Quite often, I am asked two questions about *Curious Living*:

(1) If you are constantly living in a place of wonderment,

and "unknowing" how do you "know" what to do? &

(2) How do you ever get answers to your questions, if you' re always asking questions?

ANSWERS= FOLLOW YOUR ENERGY

As children, we are conditioned to answer questions and are rewarded for having the "right" answer. I know personally, my children are always being asked and rewarded for knowing their numbers, letters etc. For their intellectual development, being able to answer questions is vital to their growth as productive human beings. Unfortunately, that "reward for answers" conditioning spills over into their spiritual, emotional or subconscious mind as well. As time goes on, you, them, me, become more conditioned to "find answers" in an effort to reap the rewards of being "right".

You probably have already concluded that you "had" the answers to all of the questions above, right? You went straight to the conclusion, that if you have a question, you must immediately have an answer, AND that answer has to show up the way you have concluded it should

Your conclusions about (a) what the answer is and (b) how it should show up, has foreclosed ALL other possibilities. The conclusion, opinion or judgment, stops the receiving of all the ways the Universe can deliver it. Your conclusions lead only to your finite understanding of what is possible for you based ONLY on what you have seen and experienced.

Now I ask you, which is bigger, you or the universe? A question is an energetic "YES" to receiving from Source, God, Shinto, Your Higher Self, (whatever resonates with you). By asking an expansive question, you have expanded your capacity to receive. In other words, you have stepped into the energetic flow to allow yourself the goodies you desire.

Your answer is your energy, your unique truth- go with ENLIGHTENMENT. Meaning, when you follow what makes you feel light and expansive, that is the result that will be created.

Ask and you shall receive, is a universal law. It works every time without fail. Every question that you ask, the Universe, summons all of the quantum entanglements to come together, just for you. If Ask and You Shall Receive is a universal law, and works EVERY time, then it will follow that you will ALWAYS receive an answer to your question.

We find what we expect to find, and we receive what we ask for." Elbert Hubbard

Where many people get tripped up, is how the answer "looks". Somehow we have in mind that the answer will be "revealed" or presented to us, like answers that come in completing a math problem or spelling a word. The answer you seek isn't limited by your conscious mind. It is so much greater than that. It will come in the form of energy, an energetic nudge, or inspirational spark.

For example, if I asked myself the question, "Would going to climb Mt Everest be an absolute blast for me, yes or no? Which one feels lighter, the yes or the no? I feel lighter with a no. I am not partial to that sort of cold. The takeaway here is that, a "no" can be light as well, just not a "yes"; It is not the answer that you are necessarily, but the emotion and feeling tied to the answer.

Your energetic nudge or impulse will most surely guide you to the next steps, i.e. a person to call, place to go, etc. It may not seem related to what you want, but that is why you must remain open and in the question. It could be you receive a nudge to go to your mailbox, and on the way, you see something, that answers the "next step question".

In other words, when you receive that energetic nudge of spaciousness, lightness, or expansiveness, ACT on it. For instance, you ask yourself the question, "what would it take for me to meet my soul mate?" Later that day, you "feel" like you need to go to the store, GO! It may be that you may meet your soul mate at the store, in the parking lot, when you arrive home as you are bringing in your groceries. Listen to your energetic nudge or inspirational spark. You asked the question, you are in the process of "receiving" your answer. Even after you receive the answer, ask another question like, "How can this get even better?"

Answers are a process rather than a destination. By accessing your Detector of Truth, you are able to create the space to receive. Remember, "Ask and You Shall Receive". As you are able to crack ANGLES and engage your Detector of Truth, you are able to live your unique truth from the infinite possibilities that exist in the Universe.

Rather than the frustration of "trying to figure it out", simply feel your way to the answer and then move or not move on that energy. You do not need to know how, so don't expect the answer to be about the "how". Do you even really care "how"? I know I didn't when it came to getting pregnant, staying pregnant and delivering healthy babies.

Questions are a natural fertilizer, feeding the mind with new ideas." Grace McCartland

"Curiosity will conquer fear even more than bravery will." James Stephens

Step 6. A^2 = Artist & Applause

"Every human is an artist. The dream of your life is to make beautiful art."
Miguel Ruiz

"In art the hand can never execute anything higher than the heart can inspire" Ralph Waldo Emerson

Generally, speaking, there is a special place in society for Artists. They get a "pass" on celebrating their uniqueness. In fact, it is encouraged, right?

I think Artists and societal reverence for them, is a great analogy for life. Artists have something that for so many is illusive. FREEDOM. Art is the essence of freedom, right? What makes it so freeing, is it's subjectivity, it's emphasis on individuality. As playwright and humorist Oscar Wilde noted, *"Art is the most intense mode of individualism that the world has known."*

How many times have you been at a Museum, or Art Exhibit, or perhaps even at a class in school, you saw a piece of Artwork and thought, "I don't get it?" The thing is, when you see Art and it's "just not your thing", you don't go into judgment of the Artist. You don't think, oh my gosh, the Art is ugly, therefore the Artist is ugly, bad and is an unworthy human being. You usually go, "I don't get it" and move on; this is generally true with other forms of Art as well.

Wouldn't it be amazing, if you just honored the Artist of Life that you are, and allowed others to do the same? Rather than making yourself wrong, or weird, you would simply follow your unique truth "in support of your Art".

"Thereisnomustinartbecauseartisfree". WassilyKandinsky

Do you remember those coloring books growing up that had the color keys? You know- the paint by numbers coloring books? They even have some cool ones at the various art and hobby stores, where you can get Michelangelo's Sistine Chapel, or Rembrandt's Night Watch. I know I personally, did a Voltran (a very cool cartoon lion robot) paint by numbers back in the day.

There are many historical artworks, that changed the world, and people's belief of what was possible; some pieces of Art created an "Era" in history.

Over the years, people have attempted and failed to reproduce that magic of those historic paintings. Millions of dollars have been spent on counterfeiting, and/or replication of those great paintings. No matter how much money spent though, the replication, no matter how similar (and even fooling an untrained and trained eye at times), will never be the original. Sure, they are as close to the original as could be, but it is still NOT the original. All of those masterpieces have creators. They were painted from the Artists' unique truth. This is something that is as unique to each of us as our fingerprints. Our unique truth cannot be duplicated, replicated, or mass produced. It is unique to you, and only you.

Everything in creation has its appointed painter or poet and remains in bondage like the princess in the fairy tale 'til its appropriate liberator comes to set it free.Ralph Waldo Emerson

You are an Artist and your '*Sistine Chapel*', or piece of music or '*Night Watch*' is your life. You can either paint by the numbers, always seeking to replicate, duplicate, or counterfeit someone else's work, or you can create your own, and change the world. I can paint Starry Night by the numbers, and though I am married to a Dutch man, I will never be Van Gogh. You can paint the Da Vinci's Last Supper by numbers, and you will never be Leonardo.

To be successful professionally, personally AND happily fulfilled, you cannot paint your life by numbers. Those people who are happy, financially, successful and changing the world, are those that are creating their own masterpieces.

It is one thing to derive inspiration from those before you but it is something altogether different, to think, that "if I could just be more like_____", I would be happy, I would be successful, I would be (fill in the blank)_________". What you would be, is NOT you. How can you ever be happy not being your truth, not being the YOU, you came into the world to be?

Where in your life are you painting by numbers? Are you redoing your vision board, according to a guru's new specifications? Perhaps you are meditating for 4 hours per day, as suggested by the meditation master? Are you resetting your SMART goals, or desperately searching for your "BIG WHY"? Maybe you are redoing (again) your affirmations, and intentions, to attract health, wealth and happiness? Are you living in poverty because you have bought the ANGLE that poverty is noble? Do you create problems for you to solve, because you have bought the ANGLE that you are a "problem-solver"?

What is true, is that no one on the planet can paint your life, as only you can, NO ONE! Attempting to achieve success and fulfillment with someone else's inspiration, ANGLES, dreams, or desires will keep you frustrated, struggling and on a treadmill to nowhere.

Wonderfully, when you are the Artist of your life's painting, you are able to receive and appreciate other people's Art, not from an ANGLE, but with respect for them as fellow Artist. Very cool, right?

Now, be honest with yourself, how many times, have you judged someone based on their self-expression and uniqueness? What ANGLE was in place for you, when they were merely "being" their Art?

"Painting is a faith, and it imposes the duty to disregard public opinion."
Vincent van Gogh

Be the Artist of Your Life. Paint it as wonderfully as you wish free from ANGLES, judgments, conclusions, and assumptions. It is just your Art. The only person that has to love it is you. What you will find though, is that the more you are fully expressed, the more you will inspire others to do the same.

Certainly, no person is an island, and I want to offer you something in the way of dealing with fellow "Artists". When a person you love makes a choice in favor of following his/her Art, rather than judging it, just say, "...that is interesting Art you are "being" or, "wow that is some interesting Art you are creating." I know many of you, think that may seem very simplistic, but what is true, life is that simple. Suffering, and making things hard, is optional. At any point, you can choose something else. Not like you are "wrong" for not choosing something else, but just being aware that you can choose something else.

An artist cannot fail; it is a success to be one. Charles Horton Cooley

APPLAUSE

"I celebrate myself, and sing myself." Walt Whitman
"The more you praise and celebrate your life, the more there is in life to celebrate." Oprah Winfrey

Are you someone, or do you know someone who never celebrates herself/himself? Something good happens, even if its small, and you and/or they almost hold their breath "waiting for the other shoe to drop". How many times have you heard or mentioned, "A collective sigh of relief?" To be clear, relief is NOT celebration.

Applause is about celebrating you today. Stated another way, make sure your days are filled with an abundance of YAYS, in your honor, of course. I like to say, that 5 Yays a Day Keeps the Energy Trolls away.

How many times a day, do you give yourself, a YAY ME? Are you regularly and consistently giving yourself a round of applause for just being you?

More than "self-acceptance", I submit that self-celebration/ appreciation is one of the keys to your kingdom. Are you a legend in your own shower? What would your life look like, if your day was filled with YAY!??

Celebrating and cheering for ourselves, not for "doing" anything but rather, just for being unique and true is part of being a Radical Self-Expert. To receive anything you desire, (a life of joy fulfillment and success) you have to be everything you need. What we see in ourselves, will be projected into the world. If you cannot give yourself, a "YAY ME", how could you possibly receive any goodness from the Universe?

Essentially, you are saying that your "being-ness" is not worthy of receiving. Your willingness to receive good from you, is in direct proportion to what you allow yourself to receive and expect to receive from the Universe.

You yourself, as much as anybody in the entire universe deserve your love and affection. Buddha

When you can give yourself, at least one genuine "YAY Me", there are numerous benefits. Celebrating you, raises your energetic vibration. Words have a vibration (because they are thoughts in form), which will create the things in your life.

Look at it this way, your self-worth is your net-worth. The Universe can only give you, what you are willing to receive. The amount of money, health, happiness, and fulfillment are a reflection of our own value. The more you recognize your own value, the more things of value you will bring into your life. Easy peezy lemon squeezy.

The more you say, YAY ME! The more things you will have to say YAY about.

Many gurus, speak often of "self-acceptance" being the key to transforming your life. While I certainly can appreciate the idea of self- acceptance, I submit, a more empowering energetic vibration would be APPLAUSE. Not just any Applause, but overflowing, good measure, pressed down, shaken together, running over YAY type APPLAUSE (yes, got that one from the Bible).

There is something about just giving myself an intuitive high-5 that reminds me of my power and fills me with excitement. It feels light, expansive and full of possibilities. One "YAY ME", simply makes me smile. Try it right now. Say it LOUD- YAY ME! Right on!

Imagine, being with you and only needing your approval and validation? Who would you be? Would you have more of you? Greater appreciation for all that you are? Sure you would!

What is absolutely true is the person I will be with 365 days in a non-leap year, 24 hours a day until my death, is ME! If I am not my everything who else will be? Now, I am not suggesting that you shouldn't have friends, trusted advisors, lovers, companions, or spouses. What I am suggesting is that by being your everything, you can have anything. Your relationship with you is a reflection of your inner value and worth. It makes sense right? How can you expect something or someone to be all things to you? Talk about pressure. Those friends, trusted advisors, lovers and spouses have their own lives, their own unique gifts that they have to give to the world. They have to work, or perhaps just need time alone to spend in reflection. Heck, even Jesus spent time alone before healing people. So what would happen to me, if I only felt validated and approved of ME, when others approved and celebrated me? YIKES! Every time, you cease to exist, wait or live in a state of the validation of others, you give away your personal power.

Worst yet, you become a “Say I am Good” Addict, looking for a “fix” of acceptance, love and approval from others. UGH! Funny thing about addiction, there is never ENOUGH to satisfy the need. You simply become more and more needy, until you will do damn near anything to have it.

Believe me, I laugh and give myself a “YAY Tiph” for recognizing and clearing the “stuff” I did as a “Say I am Good Addict” [or what I call SIAG syndrome]. Today, I can smile about it, but it was sooo not laughable going through it.

I risked EVERYTHING, including my life at one time, to feel “good enough” or for someone to “want me”. As previously indicated, I lost 5 beautiful, entirely perfect babies, because I didn’t listen to me, because I was suffering from SIAG (Say I Am Good) syndrome.

I chose through inaction (at times), and ANGLES, to leave myself vulnerable to financial, psychological, emotional, physical and spiritual predators. Believe me, I get it! Oh yea, I have dated the physical abusers...and yes, there was MORE than 1. I didn’t prosecute a stalker who would rather see me dead than with someone else; allowed members of my family to vilify and plain ole dog me, because I was desperate for approval. All me, all my choices. In many respects, there isn’t a whole heck of a lot that I haven’t been through or have done, at the height of my SIAG addiction.

It has been my experience, that self-appreciation/celebration is confused or misinterpreted as arrogance. Self-gratitude and arrogance are very different energetic vibrations. Selfishness has a heaviness and density to it energetically. The energy of selfishness is born out of an ANGLE rather than a place of space and expansion. Comparatively, self-love and gratitude have a lightness and expansion.

When you are celebrating you, it creates a ripple effect. Remember, everything is energy, right? The energy you give out, is the energy you receive back. At no point in your "YAY Me" are you looking outward. You aren't celebrating you, to prove that you are worthy to someone else. It isn't about anyone else at all; you are merely taking a moment to say to the universe, I have value and I am worthy of celebration just for *'being'*.

Whereas, when you are arrogant, it is about proving something, or showing someone how wonderful you are because deep down you fear you are not.

I think many of you, (particularly those raised in the Church), think it is selfish to celebrate yourself. I always found this confusing, because we are instructed to look at all that God made, and celebrate it. Boy, if I had a penny for every time I heard a pastor say, "Pride comes before the fall", I would be like a gotrillionare (yes that is a made up amount of money). Celebrate all that God made, but don't celebrate ourselves-(Confusing indeed-- I'm seeing another ANGLE, you too?

The more you celebrate you, the more you celebrate others. You pursue your passions and give permission to others through your inspiration to do the same. Your inspiration is the catalyst for someone else's success. How can you inspire, when you are not able to celebrate you? Ask yourself, would you rather have someone else and their approval or your own?

The time is now, for you to have and celebrate you.

Remember that your relationships are a mirror of the relationship you have with yourself. Be your cheerleader, ALLY, and best friend. This is particularly significant for those of us, who didn't grow up with love and appreciation. Gift yourself with you!

I am sure some of you are thinking, "but TK, there isn't a lot to celebrate about me, I have made so many mistakes." Believe me, as I have said, I have certainly been there. It has been my experience, that when someone says there is nothing to celebrate, they are not seeing the value in just "being" and is discounting small incremental experiences as less important than the big "shiny" experiences.

Certainly, you have had an experience where you just felt "something was off" and decided to not go through with the activity, right? That is a YAY Me moment. The thing is, when you celebrate your inner knowing, it will show up more clearly and powerfully. Rather, than feeling relief the bad thing didn't happen, celebrate the fact that you listened to you. YAY! Give you a round of APPLAUSE!

When I was pregnant with Bliss and Strycker, I celebrated me all day every day. I didn't wait to receive confirmation from the doctors that all was well. I made a point from hour to hour, to APPLAUD myself. Every hour that I was able to be pregnant was worthy of celebration as it was an hour closer to delivering healthy babies- even if I still had months to go before they could be delivered safely.

Self-Applause, is also about welcoming your truth and the fact that you made a choice to honor your truth. Cool, right? When you listen to YOU, give yourself a simple "YAY ME" and APPLAUSE. Don't wait for the big shiny experience before you start celebrating. Celebrate yourself, right now!

If you could live your life in 20 second intervals, how would you live? Do you want to live those last 20 seconds holding your breath, or do you want to live them, saying YAY Me, Dancing and APPLAUDING?? Isn't that a cool way to look at things?

Step 7. L= Leap Lively to the Lightness + Live in a Lab

As I am sure you noticed, 96% of this book was dedicated to addressing, 96% of you, aka the subconscious mind. Remember I said, she who holds the most mental real estate runs the country? Well now, that you have some very practical tools to get that 96% of you on board, we move to that 4% of you, the conscious mind.

LEAP- Leap Lively Towards Your Lightness

"Enthusiasm is the leaping lightning, not to be measured by the horse-power of the understanding." Ralph Waldo Emerson

"The jump is so frightening between where I am and where I want to be...because of all I may become I will close my eyes and leap!" Mary Anne Radmacher

Are you just as excited for you as I am about you being a Radical Self-Expert? As you read through this book, I am sure you had many an "aha" moments, right? So very cool!

What good would any of all of your new power be, if you didn't use it right? Now, it is time, to follow your lightness, to your unique pot of gold, whatever that is; and by follow, I mean leap with reckless abandon.

POSSIBILITIES
LIES

Motion vs. Meditation

It has been said, that motion beats meditation. For some of you, who swear by meditation, I am not saying that meditation does not have benefits. In fact, quite the opposite. It is also worth noting that I am a certified mediation instructor.

Think of things this way- Van Gogh said, when there is a voice inside your head that tells you, you cannot paint, then go and paint and the voice will be silenced. While meditation is good for quieting your mind, motion is the only way to actually change anything.

As Einstein puts it, "Nothing happens until something moves." You can know what you know, and that you know what is true, but if you don't leap towards it, nothing will change.

Of course, leaping keeps the energy trolls miles behind you. If you are already in action towards the lightness, when the troll of fear begins to show up, your forward motion will be like an overdrive gear. Think of it this way, a leap per day, keeps the energy trolls away.

When I graduated law school, I KNEW that working in a law firm was not an option. Despite what everyone said, I was like, "no thanks", don't want to work where I have to dress up every day. Seeing no other possibility, I taught college for a while, went back and got a Master's Degree, but the call of the law was still tugging at me.

So when I met my best friend FRED (a nickname I gave him), who was also an attorney, a little energetic spark was lit. Of course, I didn't know it was an energetic spark, because at that time, I didn't even know what self-awareness looked like.

Nevertheless, when he offered to help me pass the bar and I was like, "cool beans". On some level, he thought that I would work with him after passing the bar. Imagine his surprise when

I informed him, that I would open my own practice. He literally laughed at me and told me that he didn't think it was a good idea since I had NEVER practiced law before, been to court, met a client or anything else. My response, its ok, I think it would be "Cool" to have an office. I knew less than nothing, but opened my practice.

Later, when I told him I was going to hire someone, again he told me I was "nuts". Especially after I told him, I would hire someone with NO legal experience (she was in nursing school). He feigned support, but would constantly offer "helpful tips" about how I should be doing things.

Within months, I was making more money than he was. While I know he was happy for me, he was surprised for sure. Ever supportive when I needed him, he always stepped up and later he moved his office closer to me- which was very cool indeed. I LOVED buffet Fridays i.e. Fridays we went to the Buffet.

I tell this story, because he demonstrates how leaping towards the lightness will invariably work out for the good. I could to practice law, wear jeans every day, and hire someone who ultimately became one of my favorite people on the planet.

In fact, check this out. She met her husband because she worked for me. Seriously! Had she not worked for me, she wouldn't have met her awesome husband and had 4 beautiful children.

Leap towards the lightness ALWAYS!

"Leap and the net will appear" John Burroughs
"Many important things shouldn't be done half-way...There are times to gather your courage and make the leap, the whole leap." Jonathan Lockwood Huie

When you leap towards the lightness, the journey becomes just as fun and meaningful as the things you desire. What once seemed to be arduous and burdensome, no longer is. Rather, you are just in your energetic flow.

Imagine, being in the flow of life, with ease and joy. You are following your unique truth and correspondingly, things that may seem like work for most, are essentially play for you.

I think Thomas Edison is a shining example of leaping towards the lightness. The great inventor said, "I never did a day's work in my life. It was all fun." He is quick to point out, even of those inventions that were considered failures, "I have not failed. I've just found 10,000 ways that won't work."

Similarly, when you follow your lightness, the experience will be one of ease and play. Go towards the play!

If you want to have everything you desire, make a choice to leap towards the things that make you feel light, expansive and fluffy. I invite you to ask the question, of your choices- which choice makes you feel light and expansive and which one makes you feel heavy. Only you know for sure. No one can tell you what is true for you. In every choice you make, use the power of you, and follow your unique truth, it will only result in you being more true to you. How cool is that?

For many of us, dwelling in the heaviness of life is a sort of comfort zone (or want I like to call a limitation zone.) I am not even sure why it's called a comfort zone, because there is absolutely nothing comfortable about it. Watching other people enjoy the life that I wanted, never made me comfortable.

How about you? Do you feel comfortable in a job you despise or where you aren't feeling valued? Are you waking up every morning, thinking, "Man, this weight of the world, sure feels comfortable, I love this feeling of heaviness?" It is a zone, for sure, but comfortable it is not.

Notwithstanding, the heaviness of this zone, we stay there, right? Waiting to be rescued, or for some sort of external magic to happen to liberate us from these limitations and deliver us to the light. The rub is that the limitation barricade may keep you in, but it also keeps everything else out- hence, a life of impossibility and limitation. Think of it this way, if your comfort zone was True for you, then you wouldn't desire more.

I call it the limitation zone, because it keeps you locked up and not able to see and experience what is possible for you. Even though it is a place of lack and discontent, at least it's "familiar", right? So, we just complain, suck it up, and tell ourselves, we will "try" and be different tomorrow. I get it, historically, a comfort zone was needed for us to survive- but that was many millennia ago. Thankfully, we have evolved, and can now, make a choice to move outside the zone anytime we wish.

Heaviness is a lie, remember? Does it feel light as a feather, wanting something that is but a few steps beyond the comfort zone and not going to get it? The only way to your lightness, is to leap outside of the "comfort zone".

It is also important to note, that the point of leaping is to create dynamic change and align all of the synchronicities in the universe- just for you.

Knowledge without action, is well, just an idea, right? Some people often say, you have to have all of your ducks in a row before you make a decision and GO. I am sure you have either said that or heard that. Is that really true? Generally, when people make that statement it's because they are following the heaviness which you now understand is a lie and they are trying to manage the heaviness.

The cool thing is, when you follow the lightness, in an energy of genuine curiosity and expansive questioning, you don't need to have your ducks in a row. All of the quantum entanglements necessary for you to have the experience you seek, will align, just for you. Remember, you don't need to see 3 steps ahead, just take one step and allow the lightness to be your guide. The lightness will lead you to the next step, opportunity, or person you need to meet or connect with, to have the object(s) of your desires.

"All growth is a leap in the dark, a spontaneous, unpremeditated act without benefit of experience." Henry Miller

I am sure that you noticed that I said LEAP and not walk, or move or think about it, right? As I said, inspired motion may prove more effective that mediation in creating lasting change. That just makes sense, right? You can think about doing something all day long, use your Detector of Truth, so you know what feels light to you, but until you leap towards the lightness, nothing will change. Your light is your guide... when you leap towards it, you are on the path of your unique enLIGHTenment. You don't need to know, 5 steps ahead, you only need to go to the lightness, and that is the result that will be created. You would not feel the lightness, if it was not there to light and illuminate something exclusively just for you. So LEAP!

Do you know someone, or are you that someone who has been told to do something that you knew felt heavy, because it was your job to bring lightness to it? I know that I have and can think of at least 5 clients right now, who recently went through such a scenario.

For example, a client named Tina (not her real name), was told to "hang in there" with a guy who was driving her nuts, because he just needed a "good woman" to bring out the "good man", deep down inside. She often found herself feeling badly, because everyone said he was "right" for her, but it felt so "wrong" for her. It had gotten so bad, she started questioning whether something was wrong with her, that she "was not feeling this dude".

I invited her to ask some questions of her Detector of Truth, and note how she felt. She noted the energy that was coming up as a result. It was not light for sure. In fact, as I watched her on Skype, I noticed a physical change in her posture and her head.

After a few choice words for those that were encouraging her to follow a lie (the heaviness), and a clearing of the energy, she leaped toward the lightness, and told the guy she wouldn't remain in relationship with him. I mean, she LEAPED! I was still on Skype with her while she was calling him on the phone. After she let go of the heaviness, cleared the energy and asked some empowering questions, within a couple of days, she met the guy to whom she is now engaged. Needless to say, her friends thought she was crazy for not staying with the first guy who drove her nuts. However, she followed the lightness and the result was the beautiful relationship she always wanted.

In the interest of absolute clarity, thinking and planning to leap towards the lightness, is NOT leaping. What you want to see, is something objective. So, ask yourself, as you move towards the light each day- how many of my actions can be outwardly perceived by others? Again, planning and thinking about it, are not readily observable by anyone but you. In other words, if you were watching you, would you be able to identify specific actions taken towards your lightness.

Leaping towards the lightness works for love, money, babies (in my case) and anything else you want to experience in your life. The next step, next person you need to connect with, or next opportunity will be in the lightness.

Live in a Lab

"The opposite of nature is impossible Every time man makes a new experiment he always learns more. He cannot learn less." R. Buckminster Fuller

"Change and growth take place when a person has risked himself and dares to become involved with experimenting with his own life." Herbert Otto

When you think of a science lab, what comes to mind? Do you see people in white coats and goggles... beakers, bottles, various colors, smells, and stations? Things being mixed together to form new colors, new smells, perhaps even tastes? What you see is action, right? People, aren't just sitting around, staring at beakers. They are actively engaged in the creation of something. Adding, subtracting, mixing, taking notes. Testing, retesting, and taking more notes.

Much akin to living curiosity, experimentation creates possibilities. When you live your life as a laboratory, you are able to tailor make your life just for you. There are no rules, and nothing is set in stone.

What I mean is...some of you will find that personal growth strategy, modality or guru speaks to your truth; some of their stuff "feels true" for you and at the same time some feels heavy. Take the true "stuff" and leave the rest. Mix and match. You don't have to buy the whole outfit so to speak. It is perfectly natural to patch together a philosophy that supports your uniqueness.

I get it, believe me, I have my "favorites". I have the biggest guru crush ever on Mike Dooley from Notes from the Universe. I think he is one of the most beautiful men alive. However, I don't limit myself to his books, or teachings. I receive everything and use my Detector of Truth and then act on the lightness.

Take a little of this, and a dab of that from life, and see what you can come up with. I find that when I want to be inspired and smile, my guru crush is perfect for that. Other times, I may seek out some other modality. When I want some soul sister mother tough love, maybe I will pick up a little Iyanla Vanzant. I invite you to consider that as an infinite being, you are constantly evolving and growing. Growth demands that you be in the flow of your life. Everything that you leap towards in furtherance of discovering your true self, may be of service to you.

Let's say, you pick up a book, or go to a workshop, or buy a home study course. Portions of that book may make you feel light as a feather. Other portions may feel quite heavy. Add those things that make you feel light, to your Self-Expert repertoire and discard the rest.

By adding, subtracting, tasting, testing, you are engaged in your life. You have your Detector of Truth, which empowers you to know that you are THE EXPERT in your life, and everything else is simply information. You are not wrong for choosing something else, you are not bad because you disagree, and you aren't broken because a modality didn't work. That is the beauty and magic of being a Self-Expert. It allows you to BE YOU, an infinite BEING, powerful beyond measure, here to be a gift and contribution to the world and receive all of the goodies it has to offer. As a Self-Expert, you don't need to waste another moment of time, judging yourself because you aren't like a guru, or being unhappy trying to carry around heaviness. You are able to build upon what is true for you, in a way that is efficient and effective and move on to the next thing.

"The true method of knowledge is experiment." William Blake

Create your own YOU-unique S.Y.S.T.E.M.

S.Y.S.T.E.M perfectly encapsulates the idea of your life as a laboratory. **Save Yourself Time Energy and Money.** When you know what's true for you, don't waste your time energy or money on things that aren't true.

In other words, as the Artist of your life, if you want to paint with oils, chalk, charcoal, water colors, crayons, dirt, leaves, and a pen and it works for you, right on! GO with that.

There are no rights or wrongs. You are just experimenting. If you find that the pen is no longer serving your lightness, stop using it. It is ok! This is YOUR painting YOUR life. You are the expert on you.

"All life is an experiment. The more experiments you make the better." Ralph Waldo Emerson

By now you are already experiencing the massive shifts that come with developing your Self-Expertise with the RADICAL method.

To Recap:

Step1: Reality Nouveau

"You never change things by fighting the existing reality. To change something, build a new model that makes the existing model obsolete." Richard Buckminster Fuller

Reality \rē al i tē-\ n. The State or Quality of Being Real

Nouveau \nū'vō, nū-vō'\, adj. Newly or recently created, developed or come into prominence.

Imagine YOUR Reality Nouveau where you are the expert in your life, make the right decisions for you with ease and confidence, retire your self-sabotaging behaviors, thoughts, feelings and actions, supercharge your true potential, & stop coming up short trying to be like everyone else, and knock it out of the park, being your TRUE SELF.

Ignite your personal revolution to claim what is rightly yours, YOUR TRUTH and become the Master of Your Life.

Step 2: ANGLES

You may have heard the word ANGLE used in journalism to refer to a journalist's point of view; his/her slant or take on the story.

ANGLES are very defined, in scope, direction, perception, and can always be measured and more powerful than the limiting beliefs. This is precisely, the effect ANGLES have on the possibilities to live, have and be, everything we deserve and desire.

Think of your ANGLES as a barricade or electric doggy fence... You can't move beyond them no matter how hard you try or are desperate too. ANGLES limit your possibilities which then limit your opportunities. They are powerful because ANGLES can be both negative and positive. Think about it, if you believe, something is positive would you change it? What if though, there is something even greater than that positive thing? You wouldn't be able to see the "even better" that lies beyond the good. Great is beyond good, for a reason, you know?

We "buy" other people's ANGLES by aligning, agreeing, resisting, or reacting to them, in any way. It could be conscious, by judging something as either "right" or "wrong", "good or bad", or accidentally, as the case with aligning with our caregivers and family members.

-97% ANGLES and points of view and ANGLES, ARE NOT our own. Everyone is born ANGLE-Less. Perspectives and points of view are programmed via external factors, such our family legacy, beliefs, thoughts, religious affiliations, AKA ANGLES of INFLUENCE (hereinafter the AOI).-ANGLES have an energy and emotional charge. Science tells us that everything in the Universe is energy, including our thoughts. William Atkinson, author of Thought Vibration, said, "Many of the "stray thoughts" which come to us are but reflections or answering vibrations to some strong thought sent out by another." Our minds are receiving these thoughts and believing them to be our own, because we are vibrating on the same or similar frequency to receive it. -Locked in place in the subconscious mind by our judgments, answers, conclusions, assumptions, suppositions, and the like.

GOOD NEWS: You don't need to know the specific situation, circumstance, occurrence, relationship, or origin of the ANGLE to crack, shift, or release it.

STEP 3: DE-WAY & Detector of Truth

D – The De-Way

The De-WAY is EASY, INSTANT and POWERFUL! It is a sort of energetic detox. When you use the DE-WAY with a particular ANGLE, issue, belief, limitation, judgment, conclusion, it literally flushes the energetic charge from your body and space.

-Don't need the details of where the ANGLE came from, whose it is, or how it was locked in the place. You just need to ask and be willing to release it.

"De prefix has its origins in Latin loanwords used to form verbs that denote motion or conveyance down from, away or off; reversal or undoing of the effects of an action; extraction or removal of a thing; thoroughness or completeness of action"

> Magic words: Whatever, wherever, whenever, and ALL that this is, everywhere that I created and destroyed myself from it, through all time, space and realities, I choose now to De-create it, De-Value and Delete It. Inhale in for 5, release for 5. At the end of the breath, say aloud, YAY ME, YAY ME, YAY ME!

De-create- "De-creating" generates a new flow of expansive energy of possibility. You are both acknowledging yourself as the creator of your life, and are making another choice. You reversing or undoing the effects that you created because of your ANGLE.

De-Value- By stating that you De-Value, whatever that energy is, and everything underneath it, you are releasing whatever that ANGLE means to you and all of the value that you were attaching to it.

De-lete is from the Latin, delere which is to wipe out or destroy. By definition it means to eliminate especially by blotting out, cutting out or erasing. What you are doing by deleting all that energy that comes up in and around a particular thing, that is limiting you, or not allowing you to receive, is to erase it.

Step 4: "I" FIRST Thinker and Intuition

"I" FIRST Thinker

"To find yourself, think for yourself." – Socrates

What I am inviting you to do, is to take a moment, feel what's true and receive those thoughts, because those are YOUR thoughts.

Don't be a Bison going over the cliff.

IN-tuition vs. **OUT**-tuition

"Your mind knows only some things. Your inner voice, your instinct, knows everything. If you listen to what you know instinctively, it will always lead you down the right path." Henry Winkler

Some people refer to things like the Ego, super-ego and the like. I found it much more helpful to speak more plainly, and so, for me, there is IN-tuition and Out-Tuition.

In-tuition is my inner knowing and always originates from within and Out-tuition is everything else.

--OUT-tuition focuses on the "how", rather than my "why".

Step 5: CURIOSITY and Curious Living

"Sometimes questions are more important than answers." Nancy Willard

"It is not the answer that enlightens, but the question." Eugene Ionesco

"Ask and You Shall Receive?" It is one of the truths of the Universe. Although the principle of "Ask and You Shall Receive" is generally associated with a passage in the Bible, it is invariably a universal law.

Curiosity-consistently and continuously asking and living via empowering questions without necessarily going directly to the answer.

Step 6: A^2 Artist and Applause

ARTIST

"There is no must in art because art is free". Wassily Kandinsky

Artists and societal reverence for them, is a great analogy for life. Artists have something that for so many is illusive. FREEDOM.

To be successful professionally, personally AND happily fulfilled, you cannot paint your life by numbers. Those people who are happy, finally successful and changing the world, are those that are creating their own masterpieces.

APPLAUSE

"The more you praise and celebrate your life, the more there 's in life to celebrate." *Oprah Winfrey*

Applause is about celebrating you today. Stated another way, make sure your days are filled with an abundance of YAYS, in your honor, of course.

Look at it this way, your self-worth is your net-worth. The Universe can only give you, what you are willing to receive. The amount of money, health, happiness, and fulfillment are a reflection of our own value.

Step 7: Leap towards the Lightness

"Enthusiasm is the leaping lightning, not to be measured by the horse-power of the understanding." Ralph Waldo Emerson

Motion beats meditation and creates momentum. Leaping creates the dynamic change and aligns all of the synchronicities in the universe- just for you!

As Einstein puts it,

"Nothing happens until something moves."

What I am inviting you to do, is to take a moment, feel what's true and receive those thoughts, because those are YOUR thoughts.

REMEMBER

You can never see what is possible for you when you are walking in or living someone else's truth

There is a vitality, a life force, an energy, a quickening, that is translated through you into action, and because there is only one of you in all time, this expression is unique. Martha Graham

Your truth is as unique as your fingerprints and the only lasting path to all of the goodies you were born to receive and your greatest most reliable infallible perfect asset.

BE HAPPY TODAY!
THE EASY WAY
Opportunities
Possibilities
CHANGE YOUR LIFE NOW!
BE YOUR TRUE SELF!
1
2
3
4
5
6
7
100 mph
TRUE SELF

Acknowledgments

Where do I begin? I haven't experienced true love from a lot of people in my life, but I have experienced TONS of Love from a few people... Growing up the way I did, I had no idea what love was. All I knew was I didn't want to be me. Some people have come into my life that showed me, that being me was all they wanted and needed. I am so Blessed.

To My Angels: Not a day goes by that I don't think about you. I know you are watching over Bliss, Strycker and Spring and I am grateful that you are their protectors.

To The Royals, My Natives- Bliss, Strycker, Spring and Anchor - You are PURE Joy. I still can't believe you are mine and I get to keep you. I am sooo in love with you. I finally know what it's like to experience pure unadulterated love. Your kisses and hugs are better than Crème Brule [heaven on a plate]! I love you beyond the stars, past the moon, around the world and back again. You are the most beautiful things I have ever seen, held, touched or experienced. What else is possible?

To Guadalupe Ruiz Argleben AKA Farnsworth- What can I say? I love you beyond the moon. From the moment you walked in my office, I was your T-Diddy and You were my Farnsworth and I have been Blessed ever since. You have ALWAYS been true to me. Diddy and Farnsworth... Always and Forever [Napoleon Dynamite voice]. You always let me know that I was enough and then some.

When the "fam" was mean to me, you became my "fam". Thank you! Thank you! Through all of those losses, you kept loving me and telling me I deserved babies, that I deserved love and that God loved me. When it seemed that no one in the world loved me, YOU DID! You always filled the gap and held the space for what could be possible. I am sooo proud of you and it fills my heart to love you. You are my Diddy of Motherhood! You rock on sooo many levels. I know that God loves me, because he allowed me to experience your love. Thank you for being my Ally, thank you for always choosing to love me. I VALUE YOU!

F. Edward Harrigan AKA F.R.E.D - Thank you for stepping in when I was hurting so badly. You were the first person to show that "acting out" was not in my best interest. You lovingly, called me out, and then got me help at your expense. As I moved through the after effects of my childhood traumas and crazy choices, you were there seeing beyond the madness. You saw me... and you have always seen me. I always feel safe with you and for someone like me that is a gift of epic proportions. Thank you for socks, Tahitian pearls, counsel, lots of food, laughs, Vermont, Monster's Ball and beyonds. "You're the bomb boy, just keeping it real boo"...Thank you for being my best friend. Luv U

Thank you Noriel Molenilla... aka "Sunshine". You are an amazing graphic artist and a spectacular human being. You are "good people Sunshine". Thank you!

Achleigh-Ambur Gabrelle- "Harpo, I need you to come down here and hold this baby"... You have blossomed into quite an interestingly, funny, and independent young lady. Celebrate you every day Percy because you are worth celebrating! I love you Agent Sterling.

Thank you to all of my fellow creators from Facebook. I was hesitant to join Facebook but met some incredible people that I am proud to call my friends...

Thank you to all of the wonderful beings that have trusted me to facilitate and guide you to the beautiful beings that was always there inside of you. It is my honor and privilege to witness your manifestations, creations, transformations and actualizations. YAY!

Thank you Vid Raijn for the wonderful illustrations for this book and bringing my vision to life... you are a Serbian Picasso and a pleasure to work with. PS If anyone wants to check out his other works here is a link: www.vidrajin.tumblr.com

For more information on The RADICAL Yay-The Easy Way Gold Circle, contact me at my personal email address: Tiphanie@TheYayMeUniversity.com

You can connect with me and other *YAY'ers* on our: Facebook Page here: http://Facebook.com/TheYayMeUniversity or on Twitter @TiphanieJamEsq

Please connect with me further at: TheYayMeUniversity.com

For more support in developing your RADICAL Self-Expertise so you can become the ROCKSTAR of Your Own Life, contact me at Tiphanie@TheYayMeUniversity.com or (760)565-3106

About the Author

"Your Truth is as unique as your fingerprints and you will never see what is truly possible for you, when you are looking through or walking in someone's truth..."

An in demand coach, trainer, author and speaker, Tiphanie "TK" Jamison VanDerLugt has cracked the code of traditional personal development, with her innovative process for creating immediate life-changing results by expanding what's truly possible for your life when you become a Self-Expert. Instead of positive thinking and affirmations, she is facilitating RADICAL Self EdYOUcation as the founder of The Yay Me University™- to women (+ cool men) around the world who are tired of failing and struggling to experience the life they desire (all of life's goodies) trying to be like everyone else and are finally ready to succeed, win, be happy and have wealth being their True Self. As the World's #1 True Self Facilitator, the guiding principle in all of her work, is, "...your truth is as unique as your fingerprints and the only path to true happiness, health, wealth, ease and infinite possibilities. Since possibilities create opportunities, how many opportunities will you miss, because someone else says it's not possible? You will never see what is possible for you, walking in or looking through someone else's truth." At The Yay Me University™, you are guided to discover your true self, so you boost your true wealth and live happily with days filled with YAY- the Easy Way.

Her book, "The Radical Self-Expert" was born out of her recognition that traditional personal development methods were not working and left her and countless others feeling like personal development misfits. Her method supercharges the discovery of your true self by playfully and powerfully inviting you to experience creating and generating a life and living that You LOVE, FREE from judgments and limitations, so you take bold actions + get rapid unprecedented results in any area of your life that isn't working as you desire it to. "Who would you be if you lost your ability to judge you... If you lost your ability to receive the judgments of others about you and make them your own?" asks, Tiphanie. She facilitates a one of a kind interactive RADICAL Self-Expert Experience virtually and in person to thrilled audiences around the world. Although it was not until her adulthood, that she welcomed her "misfit-ness", her commitment to "write your own rules, so you always win" attitude can be seen throughout her life. In the face of childhood abuse and neglect, she begin college at the age of 15, taught college and university courses with no experience in her early 20's and opened a successful solo law practice with no training, mentors, or business experience.

Tiphanie developed and created 2 definitive laudable self-assessment tests: The True Self Test (also known as the True Self IQ Test) and The True To Self-Test.

She has authored 3 books for print, The RADICAL Self-Expert, The Book on the True Self, The Book on the Pregnancy After Loss and the upcoming The Book on How to Pass the Bar.

Her formal education includes a Bachelors in Criminal Justice and Masters of Science in International Relations and a Juris Doctor; All of which she completed by the age of 27. For a copy of her academic credentials, please send your request to Support@TheYayMeUniversity.com. She is also a certified hypnotist, meditation master and nlp certified practitioner. Tiphanie is a licensed attorney for the 9th Federal District and the State of California.

A bit quirky and more tomboy than she appears, Tiphanie's profound intellect and vibrancy, make for an adventurous and imaginative environment, in which self-growth is more delightful than difficult. She is a fun, passionate, sports jock who celebrates her feminine curves, and loves soft rock music from the 70s and 80s.

Want to Create The RADICAL YAY Experience ?

If you have you gotten your hands on this book (digitally or paperback), one thing I know about you, is that you are looking for a fresh, FUN, energetic, dynamically life- changing perspective brimming with the right combination of "woo woo + go and do" to create instant and lasting transformative value for others.

Host Tiphanie at an Event, Workshop, Chapter Meeting, Fundraiser or Group…

Do you have access to a group, chapter meeting, workshop or fundraiser of women + cool men, who want to experience DAYS, Filled with YAY- the Easy Way??? Tiphanie is available to FACILITATE the RADICAL SELF-Expert Experience. The Experience is ALL interactive and completely customized to your event. There is no "one size fits all" with anything Tiphanie does. Gift your audience with epic value and experience a revolutionary system that your event- goers will use for the rest of their lives to create stellar success- financially, spiritually and globally with their unique gifts, talents and passions. Inspiration + Education +

Entertainment + Motion= YAY! The Easy Way!

Thought-provoking, humorous, transcendent and a BLAST... If you are ready, willing and excited to bring something innovative and new to your event, please contact Tiphanie directly at Tiphanie@TheYayMeUniversity.com or by telephone at (760) 565-3106. Fees may apply depending on your audience, event and location.

Endnotes

1. Wood, Joanne V., W.Q. Elaine Perunovic, and John W. Lee. "Positive Self-Statements: Power for Some, Peril for Others." Psychological Science 20.7 (2009): 860-66. Print.
2. ID at 865. Print.
3. Seven Costly Pro Athlete Screw-ups." *Yahoo! Sports*. Web. <http://sports.yahoo.com/top/news?slug=ys-investopediamoneyloss031010>.
4. "Nikola Tesla." Wikipedia, the Free Encyclopedia. <http://en.wikipedia.org/wiki/Nikola_Tesla>.
5. Add it later.
6. Random Webster's Dictionary
7. Id.
8. "Beta-endorphin." *Wikipedia*. Wikimedia Foundation, 01 Jan. 2012. Web. 22 Apr. 2012. <http://en.wikipedia.org/wiki/Beta-endorphin>.
9. "Dopamine." *Wikipedia*. Wikimedia Foundation, 19 Apr. 2012. Web. 22 Apr. 2012. <http://en.wikipedia.org/wiki/Dopamine>.
10. Binazir, Dr. Ali. "Addiction Recovery: Why We're Addicted to Negative Behaviors." The Huffington Post. TheHuffingtonPost.com, 17 Nov. 2011. Web. 01 Jan. 2012. <http://www.huffingtonpost.com/dr-ali-binazir/addiction-recovery-why-we_b_603566.html>.
11. "Cortisol." *Wikipedia*. Wikimedia Foundation, 19 Apr. 2012. Web. 01 Jan. 2012. <http://en.wikipedia.org/wiki/Cortisol>.

12. Binazir, Dr. Ali. "Addiction Recovery: Why We're Addicted to Negative Behaviors." *The Huffington Post.* TheHuffingtonPost. com, 17 Nov. 2011. Web. 01 Jan. 2012. <http://www. huffingtonpost.com/dr-ali-binazir/addiction-recovery-why- we_b_603566.html>.

13. Webster's.

14. "Buffalo Jump." Wikipedia, the Free Encyclopedia. Web.<http://en.wikipedia.org/wiki/Buffalo_jump>.

15. Carlin Flora. "Gut Almighty". Psychology Today. Vol 40. Issue 3:68-75,2007.

www.ingramcontent.com/pod-product-compliance
Lightning Source LLC
LaVergne TN
LVHW051123080426
835510LV00018B/2207

* 9 7 8 0 6 1 5 7 4 2 6 6 3 *